The North Mexican Cattle Industry, 1910–1975

The North Mexican Cattle Industry, 1910–1975

Ideology, Conflict, and Change

By Manuel A. Machado, Jr.

Texas A&M University Press, *College Station*

Library of Congress Cataloging in Publication Data

Machado, Manuel A
    The north Mexican cattle industry, 1910–1975.

        Bibliography: p.
        Includes index.
        1. Cattle trade—Mexico—History I. Title.
    HD9433.M62M33   338.1'76'009721   80-5515
    ISBN 0-89096-104-2

Manufactured in the United States of America
FIRST EDITION

For Terry, lifelong amigo,
who also toils in the educational vineyard

Contents

List of Illustrations

Preface

¡¡Cuernos, cuero y cojones!!—Not a flattering description of the cattle that roamed the vast desert ranges of northern Mexico from the sixteenth through most of the nineteenth centuries. But environmental demands forced the descendants of the proud bulls and haughty cows of Andalusía to adapt to harsh surroundings in northern Mexico: they became fleet of foot, their already prodigious horns grew even longer as they battled against predators, and the Longhorns' capacity for survival in the immense tracts of Mexico resulted in an astonishing reproduction rate.

Gregorio Villalobos landed the first cattle in Mexico in 1521; the development of cattle ranching accompanied that of Mexico as Spanish control spread from its center, Mexico City. By the 1560's, Spanish hegemony extended into the far north. Zacatecas and Coahuila came under full Spanish control. The large *haciendas*, developed originally as a means of supplying the mines of northern Mexico, became semiautonomous socioeconomic units as the mineral deposits played out. Their vast expanses, predicated upon the extensive use of range land, supported thousands of *peones* and produced millions of cattle. Tracts reached into the millions of acres; thus, although nominally under the control of man, the feral Longhorn saw little of his domesticator.

Within the milieu of the cattle hacienda developed a fierce independence and a reluctance to truckle to the demands of an overweening government. The remoteness of the northern haciendas from Mexico City allowed the *hacendados*, or large ranchers, to conduct their affairs with little or no external interference by centralized authority. This, of course, does not mean that the imperial government of Spain or, later, the various shaky national governments of the nineteenth century did not seek to circumscribe the independence of the hacendados; but distance made communication difficult, and the control of the north by Mexico City remained tenuous and resulted more from *norteño* nationalist loyalties than from actual government power.

This study focuses upon the persistence of hacienda culture in northern Mexico despite the revolutionary onslaughts of the period 1910–1930, the accelerated reformism of the 1930's, and the institutional revolution of the period after 1946. Mexico's cattle production dropped more than 60 percent between 1910 and 1923; yet the country slowly regained its role as a producer of fine cattle, cattle worthy of export not only to the United States but also to other parts of Latin America. This regeneration has occurred despite the fact that, from the period of the Revolution on, government action aimed at the dismantling of large landholdings. Mexico's Constitution of 1917 incorporated and thus legitimized an attack on the large haciendas. Yet, even today, cattle in northern Mexico remain the product of large landholdings (though much reduced from the days of Luis Terrazas), improved technology and techniques of husbandry, and a persistent norteño individualism that circumvented with partial success the encroachments of centralized authority in Mexico City. Perhaps the unavailability of data on the sizes of individual holdings in northern Mexico also reflects the central government's "levelling" policy: the Dirección General de Estadística, in its compilation of the *Anuarios estadísticos*, differentiates only holdings of less than five hectares from those of more than five.

The accident of geography rather than the intentions of government seems to be responsible for the continuing prosperity of northern Mexico's cattle industry. The ready market for feeder cattle in the United States has created a dependency of north Mexican cattlemen on United States buyers. By the same token, operators of feedlots in the United States have come to depend on Mexican producers of quality feeder stock. Thus, mutual dependency has drawn the cattlemen of Mexico and the United States Southwest closer together in a common effort to produce cattle for the demanding United States market.

The conceptual blending of science (animal husbandry), history, and diplomacy poses a challenge for the student of United States–Mexican relations. In the first place, the diplomatic historian must possess not only the language skills necessary for the usual documentation of history but also a functional scientific bilingualism. In addition, the historian who enters the two areas of science and diplomacy needs either some training in the sciences or an affinity for a branch of the sciences with which he is dealing. Finally, even experience with pungent corrals and heady laboratory smells does not adequately prepare the historian for an investigation of the role of disease in history. Rather, the scholar must be committed to the idea that diplomatic history amounts to more than the exchange of notes between chancelleries and the arousal of the political passions of various constituencies.

This study has evolved from long interest in the cattle industry of Mexico and of the United States. Charges of being a frustrated cowboy and of being occasionally redolent of the farm have not diminished that interest. Early graduate work in the history of livestock disease control as a diplomatic factor between Mexico and the United States provided a starting point for larger consideration of the Mexican cattle industry in the twentieth century. I owe many thanks to the late Donald M. Dozer, my mentor at the University of California at Santa Barbara, who encouraged me to pursue my own interest; this work owes much to his tutelage. The result: a frustrated cowboy who claims to be a historian but who raises Arabian horses, teaches his sons to rope in the hope that they can become rodeo champions and therefore support the old man, and prefers living in the country to the genteel amenities of a university town.

Other academic mentors have supported me in my pursuit of Mexican cows. Philip Powell and Lawrence Kinnaird, both of the University of California at Santa Barbara, in their respective ways continued to urge me into avenues that were as yet unexplored.

During the initial phases of this study, Tom Fulton, then a graduate student at the University of Montana, served as my research assistant. In spite of culture shock in Washington, D.C., Tom performed exemplary service in the research for this work. Washington, D.C., no longer shocks Tom. He works there as a historian in the Agricultural History Branch of the Department of

Agriculture. To him goes immeasurable gratitude for his assistance in this project.

Funding remains an essential ingredient in the pursuit of historical knowledge. The Social Science Research Council provided a generous grant that allowed me to travel and to conduct my research in 1971–1972. Since then no further travel has been absolutely necessary, though I continue to take every opportunity to get to Mexico.

Chapter 1 and portions of chapter 2 originally appeared in the *Southwestern Historical Quarterly* and *Agricultural History*, respectively. Thanks are due to both journals for permission to reprint the material. Portions of chapter 4 appeared in my earlier work, *AFTOSA: Foot-and-Mouth Disease and Inter-American Relations* (Albany: State University of New York Press, 1969). To them also I extend thanks for permission to reprint.

Typing epitomizes drudgery for me. Ms. Jeanie Anderson of the history department suffered through the manuscript and typed it in final form. She too is deserving of thanks.

Finally, my family must be mentioned. They have tolerated the absences, the pecking away at the typewriter, and the generally nasty tempers growing from frustration that accompany the preparation of any study. To them and especially to my wife Marcy, go my thanks for their understanding and tolerance.

No one else is responsible for this work. What errors exist must fall squarely on my shoulders, and I accept the responsibility gladly.

The North Mexican Cattle Industry, 1910–1975

Prologue: Dawn of Revolution

BUZZARDS circled lazily over the barren Chihuahua desert as they searched for carrion on which to gorge themselves. Below, on the desert floor, occasional scrawny cattle picked at the sparse vegetation while a brown, dusty *vaquero* mounted on a stunted horse gently guided the stock toward a collection of crudely constructed cattlepens. It is a rugged land, a land unfit for survival by any but the toughest of men, women, and animals. Early settlers in Chihuahua during the seventeenth and eighteenth centuries required a hardiness of spirit that might well have baffled colonizers in other parts of Mexico, for the inimical environment could appeal only to those sufficiently hardy to tolerate the extremes of wind, cold, heat, and aridity.[1]

As the colonization of New Spain extended northward, the haciendas in the north grew. On them was created a social system of mutual dependency between the *patrón* and his peones. Vast tracts of land controlled by single families dominated social and economic life. Hacienda culture revolved around reasonably self-sufficient economic units with minimal dependence on outside sources for materials and labor. The major economic pursuits on the haciendas were sheep and cattle. Haciendas of over 3 million

---

[1] Information for the prologue comes from the following works: Florence C. Lister and Robert H. Lister, *Chihuahua: Storehouse of Storms*; Diego G. López Rosado, *Historia y pensamiento económico de México, Agricultura y ganadería: Propiedad de la tierra*, I; Harold D. Sims, "Espejo de caciques: Los Terrazas de Chihuahua," *Historia Mexicana* 18 (January–March, 1969), 379–399; Donald D. Brand, "The Early History of the Range Cattle Industry in Northern Mexico," *Agricultural History* 35 (July, 1961), 132–139; Luis Cossío Silva, "La ganadería," in Daniel Cosío Villegas, ed., *Historia moderna de México. El Porfiriato. La vida económica*, VI, pt. 1, 135–153.

acres were not uncommon, for cattle required between 75 and 125 acres per cow-calf unit for full year-round pasturage. A vast vaquero labor force worked these cattle. Though tied to the haciendas through debt peonage, the vaqueros themselves possessed an independence of spirit not seen in other regions of Mexico.

Isolation of social units in Chihuahua and most of northern Mexico encouraged a sense of localism, a fierce loyalty to local and regional allegiances rather than to amorphous appeals to nationalism. In northern Mexico were found the fiercest detractors of excessive centralization by Mexico City.

When Mexico achieved independence in 1821, the organization of the country under a federalist constitution in 1824 included provisions for states' rights demanded by northern delegates. Having suffered too long under a centralized power during the colonial period, the northerners wanted no more interference in the management of their affairs. Consequently, tension persisted throughout the nineteenth century between northern Mexico and the central authority in Mexico City.

The harsh Chihuahua environment provided respite and support—financial, moral, and military—for Benito Juárez as he was driven northward by conservative and French forces during the French occupation of Mexico (1864–1867). Luis Terrazas, who would become the leading hacendado of northern Mexico, staunchly supported Juárez as nationalist forces regrouped and reorganized in a final drive against the French invaders and their Mexican allies.

The successful expulsion of the French in 1867 left northern Mexico open to development. Confiscation of lands belonging to French sympathizers allowed loyal hacendados to increase their holdings, accelerate their production, and enlarge their forces of peones and vaqueros. Complex marital arrangements not unlike the dynastic relationships of Europe allowed men like Luis Terrazas to expand; his family eventually controlled over 6.5 million acres of land in addition to mines, lumber companies, and banks. Between 1900 and 1910, Luis Terrazas' average annual calf crop amounted to around 70,000 calves. In 1910, he reportedly branded 140,000 calves. This astonishing number made him probably the largest single cattle owner in the world, with the exception of a corporate operation in Brazil.

In achieving their control, the hacendados of Chihuahua increased the pressure of debt peonage on the peones and vaqueros who formed the backbone of the hacienda system. In addition, demands in the United States for feeder cattle from northern Mexico not only encouraged increased production on existent haciendas but also promoted the development of United States–owned haciendas in northern Mexico whose holdings would rival those of Mexican hacendados.

Foreign ownership of these northern lands increased as Porfirio Díaz consolidated his power. By encouraging foreign capital in Mexico, Díaz opened the floodgates to foreign control of much of the national domain in a variety of enterprises: cattle, mining, railroads, public utilities, and banking. Nevertheless, Mexico found order. During the long tenure of Porfirio Díaz (1876–1911), economic progress in Mexico was undeniable. But its achievement also brought about the increased exploitation of peones on haciendas. In northern Mexico, and in Chihuahua specifically, the hacienda system kept the peones on the ranch and allowed little mobility for any but the upper strata of society.

In the early 1880's, the character of the Mexican cattle industry began to change. More and larger foreign landholdings competed with Mexican haciendas for the production of cattle for export to the United States. The demand for cattle in the United States continually pressed Mexican cattlemen to ship more stock to the border. Between 1881 and 1892, Mexico exported over 4,500,000 pesos' (about $2,225,000) worth of livestock carrying a five-year average value of 367,400 pesos per annum.

Exports of cattle increased in direct proportion to the importation of purebred stock for breed improvements. During the thirty-five years of the *porfiriato*, Mexico imported about 160,000 head of blooded cattle, the majority of them from the United States. But by 1910, there were only 700,000 head of purebred stock in Mexico, 7 percent of the total number of cattle in the country. This situation resulted partly from the persistence of lackadaisical management practices which led to dilution of the purebred strain.

Throughout Díaz' long tenure, he could not count on Chihuahua for unstinting support. Personal animosity between himself and Luis Terrazas dating back to their mutual fight against the French made Díaz wary of tangling too openly with the powerful Terrazas clan. The norteño spirit, fostered on the arid plains and in the rugged mountains of Chihuahua, continued to resist the forces of centralized government.

Díaz grew old and so did most of his supporters. Political ferment throughout the country exploded in 1910 into a revolution aimed primarily at the overthrow of Díaz but eventually resulting in almost total social and economic dislocation.

An ordered society had been created in Chihuahua, a society predicated upon a hacienda system that maintained social stability. But this sense of order proved ephemeral; after 1910, the same peones that had worked so assiduously on the large haciendas revolted against the existing order and manifested the same fierce independence that characterized their former patrones. Coupled with this independent attitude came a desire to reclaim the land on which they had worked. Joining the various revolutionary armies, peones in northern Mexico seized lands, cattle, equipment, and money belonging to the hacendados and used these either for personal aggrandizement or to further the cause of the Revolution.

Thus, northern Mexico, and especially Chihuahua—"*la cuna de la Revolución*" (the cradle of the Revolution)—gave voice early to discontent. In so doing, it precipitated a massive upheaval that threw into oblivion Mexico's social and economic structure and very nearly destroyed the northern cattle industry.

1. An Industry Destroyed, 1910–1920

REVOLUTIONARY upheaval in Mexico, beginning in 1910 and continuing into the 1920's, destroyed the flourishing beef cattle industry of the country's northern states. In the massive pillaging of extensive cattle haciendas could be found some of the impelling factors of the Mexican Revolution—a quest for land, nationalism bordering on xenophobia, foraging by revolutionary factions, and the destruction of the large haciendas and the attendant system of peonage. The conflicts affecting the Mexican cattle industry during this tumultuous decade exacerbated the already strained relations between Mexico and the United States.

Northern Mexico's cattle industry had attained major importance in the national economy by 1900. Large haciendas, developed over a span of nearly four centuries, annually produced hundreds of thousands of head of cattle that enriched northern hacendados and filled ranges in both Mexico and the United States. According to the agricultural census of 1902, the Mexican states of Coahuila, Chihuahua, Durango, Nuevo León, and Sonora contained over one million head of cattle valued at approximately twelve million pesos.[1] This industry aimed primarily at an export market in the United States; as a result, attempts were made to upgrade the quality of livestock in order to improve its market value north of the Rio Grande.

Impetus for the improvement of Mexico's *criollo*, or native, stock had come from both Mexican and foreign cattlemen. The importation of Hereford bulls by such stock raisers as the Corralitos Land and Cattle Company, a United States–based firm later owned

[1] Dirección General de Estadística, *Estadística ganadera de la República*, pp. 9, 41, 45, 49, 51. Before 1910 the peso was valued at two to the dollar.

by British interests, and Luis Terrazas, Mexico's largest landholder and former governor of Chihuahua, had produced a meatier, more valuable animal on Mexican ranges by 1910.[2] Progressive improvement of Mexican livestock had resulted in increased importation by the United States. Between 1906 and 1909, for example, approximately 150,000 head of Mexican cattle entered the United States market. During the early phases of the Mexican Revolution (1911–1912) the United States absorbed 95 percent of Mexico's exported cattle.[3]

Massive imports by United States cattlemen caused concern among officials of various United States livestock organizations. In a speech to the Texas Livestock Raisers Association in March, 1910, Ike T. Pryor, a Texas pioneer cattleman, voiced apprehension that the continued free entry of Mexican cattle would increase the cost of feed to the cattleman and thus result in higher meat prices for the consumer.[4] Pryor's objection, however, was out of step with the reality of increased importations from Mexican ranges.

The generally pleasant relationship between Mexican cattlemen and United States buyers soon deteriorated. Revolution struck Mexico with a force that paralyzed her cattle industry and made the United States suspicious of anything Mexican. The decade 1910–1920 depleted Mexico's herds and left her ranges bare and unproductive, ravaged by revolutionary and counterrevolutionary forces that took cattle for food or for sale in the United States as a means of procuring specie for the purchase of war materiel.[5]

Revolutionary upheaval in Mexico centered initially on the

[2] D. E. Salmon, *Mexico as a Market for Purebred Beef Cattle from the United States*, pp. 15–16; Donald D. Brand, "The Early History of the Range Cattle Industry in Northern Mexico," *Agricultural History* 35 (July, 1962), 132–139.

[3] "El crédito a la ganadería en Mexico," *Revista de economía continental* 2 (January, 1947), 18; Emilio Alanís Patiño, "La industria de la carne en México," *Problemas agrícolas e industriales de México* 4 (July–September, 1952), 245.

[4] Ike T. Pryor, "Is Beef on the Hoof Too High When Compared to the Cost of Production?" Ike T. Pryor Papers, University of Texas Archives, Austin, pp. 45–46.

[5] Diego G. López Rosado, *Historia y pensamiento económico de México, Agricultura y ganadería: Propiedad de la tierra*, I, 141; Florence C. Lister and Robert H. Lister, *Chihuahua: Storehouse of Storms*, p. 265.

problem of political succession. Yet the forces unleashed by Francisco Madero in 1910 sought social changes greater than political reforms. A major impulse in the Revolution was the demand for equitable distribution of land. Mixed with the desire for land was a hatred of foreign companies that possessed vast holdings.[6] Northern hacendados and their livestock became primary targets of revolutionary groups that sought to wrest control away from old-line adherents of Porfirio Díaz. During Díaz' long tenure as president of Mexico, the *latifundios,* or large landed estates, had grown rapidly. Before 1910, nineteen latifundios had controlled nearly half of Mexico's largest state, Chihuahua. Companies such as the Palomas Land and Cattle Company, a United States–owned concern immediately across the border from Columbus, New Mexico, and the Babícora Ranch of publisher William Randolph Hearst, as well as the vast holdings of Luis Terrazas, became particularly odious symbols of the old regime.[7]

The Mexican Revolution began to lose cohesion shortly after Madero took power in 1911. Splinter groups pronounced against him. One of these, headed by Pascual Orozco, Jr. (former commander of Madero's revolutionary army) and based in Chihuahua, posed a major threat to the government and thwarted Madero's feeble attempts to bring democracy to Mexico.[8] Along the Mexican border, *federales* (government troops) systematically acquired cattle and horses, by licit and illicit means, in an effort to prepare themselves for the onslaught of Orozco's *colorados.* The federales also aimed to protect United States landholdings in northern Chihuahua.[9]

[6] Ronald Atkin, *Revolution! Mexico, 1910–1920,* is an excellent study of the background and the major decade of revolutionary upheaval in Mexico.

[7] Francisco R. Almada, *La revolución en el estado de Chihuahua,* I, 58–60.

[8] For a detailed study of Orozco, see Michael C. Meyer, *Mexican Rebel: Pascual Orozco and the Mexican Revolution, 1910–1915.* Orozco was a muleskinner turned revolutionary general. He and Francisco Villa were instrumental in defeating Díaz's forces at Ciudad Juárez in 1911. Orozco broke with Francisco Madero in 1912 and led his *colorado* troops against his former leader. For a while Orozco and Huerta were opposed to each other; in 1915, however, they made common cause in an attempt to begin a counterrevolution in Mexico. See also Michael C. Meyer, *Huerta: A Political Portrait.*

[9] Luther T. Ellsworth to Philander C. Knox, March 27, 1912, Papers of the Department of State Relating to the Internal Affairs of Mexico, 1910–

Orozco recognized the economic potential that northern Mexico's cattle presented for his counterrevolution. His forces stole cattle from northern haciendas and sold them in the United States in exchange for ordnance. Mexico's Secretariat of Foreign Relations requested that the United States Department of State stop all cattle imports from rebels. Under existing statutes, however, the United States could not refuse the importation of cattle which met sanitary requirements.[10]

The *orozquista* rebellion established the pattern of forcible seizure and cattle rustling for the remainder of the Revolution. Orozquista commanders sold Mexican livestock across the border and threatened hacendados with devastation if they failed to comply with rebel demands.[11]

Within a year the Orozco rebellion was reduced to a guerrilla movement by General Victoriano Huerta. Huerta then moved against Madero and in February, 1913, arrested the president and elevated himself to the presidency. Huerta's unlawful seizure of power and the subsequent assassination of Madero precipitated a massive new rebellion against the usurper. Venustiano Carranza, governor of Coahuila, proclaimed the *Plan de Guadalupe* in March, 1913, and called on all loyal Mexicans to take arms against Huerta. Men such as Francisco Villa, Alvaro Obregón, and Pablo González joined him. Carranza's tenuous *constitucionalista* coalition resorted to many of the same tactics that Orozco had employed the previous year to finance an armed movement against the established government. Mexico's cattle ranges again yielded a source of money and arms for contending factions.[12]

1929, File 812.00/3435, Record Group 59, National Archives, Washington, D.C. Hereafter cited as RG 59, NA.

[10] Manuel Calero to Knox, June 22, 1912, File 812.00/4291; F. MacVeagh to Knox, July 1, 1912, File 812.00/4348, RG 59, NA.

[11] Ellsworth to Knox, August 31, 1912, File 812.00/4792, RG 59, NA; Estado Mayor to Secretaría de Relaciones Exteriores, September 5, 1912, L.E. 925R, Archivo Histórico de la Secretaría de Relaciones Exteriores, Tlatelolco, D.F. Hereafter cited as AHRE.

[12] Carranza's principal objective was a restoration of constitutional government, hence the name "constitucionalista" for his movement. An excellent study of the Constitutionalist movement can be found in Charles C. Cumberland, *Mexican Revolution: The Constitutionalist Years*.

Carranza's forces did not discriminate between cattle owned by *huertistas* and those owned by foreign landholders. In March and April, 1913, huertista general Gerónimo Treviño saw his hacienda in Chihuahua pillaged of nearly 2,500 head of livestock, which in turn found markets in the United States. Although United States officials in Mexico attempted to ascertain ownership of the stock, little could be done about its sale north of the Rio Grande.[13]

Carrancista pillaging continued through the summer of 1913. In mid-August, constitucionalista forces at Ciudad Porfirio Díaz (present-day Piedras Negras) avoided the United States quarantine on Mexican cattle infested with fever ticks by slaughtering the beef in Mexico and then shipping the meat into the United States. Because carrancistas controlled some of the border towns, United States residents could also cross into Mexico to purchase low-priced beef with money which augmented revolutionary coffers.[14] Such activities became typical practice for avoiding prohibitions on Mexican stock entering the United States.

Seizure of livestock continued through the fall of 1913 as Carranza's growing forces found their needs for arms and food supplies steadily increasing. In October one United States–owned cattle company in Baja California armed its men, hoping to protect cattle from seizure by revolutionaries or bandits. General Alvaro Obregón, commander of the Army of the Northwest, alleged that these men were consciously aiding Huerta and would therefore be treated as traitors. The United States consul at Ensenada, Claude C. Guizant, however, declared that "it is natural that this company should arm their several hundred employees for their own protection." He added that the move was not made with "any intention to aid the de facto Government of Mexico."[15]

The fighting against Huerta ended in July, 1914. Huerta embarked for Europe, and the tempestuous alliance between Carranza and Villa approached a rupture. Estrangement was apparent as

[13] Ellsworth to W. J. Bryan, March 24, 1913, File 812.00/6917, RG 59, NA. See also Mexican Consul, Eagle Pass, to Relaciones Exteriores, May 6, 1913, L.E. 750R, AHRE.

[14] Ellsworth to Bryan, August 9, 1913, File 611.125/8, RG 59, NA.

[15] Louis Hostetter to Bryan, October 12, 1913, File 812.00/9353; Claude C. Guizant to Bryan, November 8, 1913, File 812.00/9729, RG 59, NA.

early as April, 1914; their divergent personalities and different perspectives of the Revolution increased the rift. Disagreements, sometimes acrimonious, over political appointments in *villista*-controlled territory, the deployment of the División del Norte at Zacatecas, and Carranza's failure to supply ordnance and materiel to Villa's army magnified the personal animosity between the two leaders. Attempts to repair the revolutionary organism failed, and by mid-September Villa and Carranza were at nearly irreconcilable odds. Relations continued to deteriorate, with mutual recriminations punctuating the tension, and by October 1 open hostility seemed inevitable.

Such circumstances made the sale of confiscated cattle difficult, especially for Carranza: villistas controlled the major railhead and large slaughterhouse at Ciudad Juárez and effectively prevented carrancista shipments to El Paso.[16]

Livestock owners quickly realized that if they wanted a profit from their stock they would have to ship cattle into the United States. Such massive shipments would leave revolutionary forces without a source of money and food supplies. In late May, 1914, General Pablo González, commander of the Army of the Northeast, prohibited the private export of cattle to the United States through areas under his control. Violations were punishable by confiscation of entire herds and by one to five years' imprisonment.[17]

Throughout the struggle against Huerta and the subsequent battle between Villa and Carranza, Villa controlled Chihuahua, the principal producer of beef cattle. From March, 1913, until Villa's break with Carranza in October, 1914, villistas and other constitucionalistas seized cattle from northern haciendas. The break between Carranza and Villa, however, left the villistas to their own devices. The Convention at Aguascalientes, which had its impetus from a suggestion by Woodrow Wilson following the break between Villa and Carranza, began as an attempt to establish a form of government for Mexico. Carranza, however, refused to recognize the sovereignty of the Convention, and his representatives left with him

---

[16] Cumberland, *Constitutionalist Years*, pp: 127–131, 133–136, 138–139, 158–159.

[17] Z. L. Cobb to Bryan, October 1, 1914, File 611.125; William P. Blocker to Bryan, October 14, 1914, File 812.00/13541, RG 59, NA.

when he went to Veracruz to establish a government. Consequently, the Convention came to be dominated by villistas and *zapatistas*, with General Eulalio Gutiérrez as its president. Supported principally by Villa's troops, it became a debating society with few practical achievements. Operating from Veracruz in the fall of 1914 and aided militarily by Alvaro Obregón, Carranza eventually pushed the Convention out of Mexico City in early 1915, defeated Villa's troops, and ultimately won United States recognition in October, 1915.

Once entrenched in power, Carranza organized a government in an attempt to restore social and political order to Mexico. He did not succeed, however, in routing corruption even from his own ranks. Revolutionary chieftains capitalized upon Mexico's unsettled situation and lined their own pockets. One example, reported to the United States Department of State, involved General Francisco Murguía, a prominent carrancista. In June, 1917, Murguía answered a call for a conference with Carranza in Mexico City. Before leaving Chihuahua he shipped three trainloads (approximately 2,000 head) of cattle questionably acquired to his ranch in Zacatecas.[18]

When the Convention at Aguascalientes took an *agrarista* (agrarian-oriented) turn in November, 1914, and established a Comisión Nacional Agraria (National Agrarian Commission), villista chieftains reacted with dismay. They retained their hold on Chihuahua, occupied confiscated haciendas, and took the remaining cattle for their own use or for sale in the United States. The commission, however, in an obvious concession to the influence of Emiliano Zapata of Morelos, dispatched a group of land reformers to Chihuahua to divide the land among the peasantry. Despite the military alliance between Zapata and Villa, the northern leaders resisted the reformers as they entered Chihuahua and attempted to divide its arid land into plots similar to those farther south.[19]

---

[18] Cobb to Robert Lansing, June 4, 1914, File 812.00/20981, RG 59, NA. In Cobb to Lansing, June 11, 1917 (File 812.00/21003, RG 59, NA), Cobb reported a conference with the French consul in Chihuahua, who confirmed Murguía's pilfering.

[19] Marte R. Gómez, *La reforma agraria en las filas villistas, años 1913 a 1915 y 1920*, p. 82. For a detailed study of the Convention, see Robert E. Quirk, *The Mexican Revolution, 1914–1915: The Convention at Aguascalientes*.

Livestock raisers in Chihuahua responded to villista confiscations of their cattle by attempting to remove the stock to the United States in order to salvage at least a part of their investment. Villa imposed prohibitions upon exports, and representatives of the Department of State protested his action. Ultimately Villa relented and granted permission for the passage of old bulls, old cows, and aged steers. This limitation forced cattlemen to maintain young breeding stock on their ranges for the perpetuation of herds in the area. In addition, cattle raisers had to pay an export tax of ten dollars per head to villista authorities at ports of entry to the United States.[20]

Villa's control of Ciudad Juárez gave him a virtual monopoly on the shipment of cattle to the United States. In November, 1914, Villa seized the municipal slaughterhouse at Juárez and began remodeling it in order to comply with United States specifications for the sale of slaughtered beef. He thus avoided the quarantine on tick-infested cattle from Mexico.[21] The subsequent history of the slaughterhouse demonstrated the capriciousness of United States policy vis-à-vis Villa, by which livestock exports from Mexico were used as pawns in President Woodrow Wilson's attempts to regulate the Revolution.

Seizure of the Juárez slaughterhouse failed to net Villa an instant source of funds. With the initial villista takeover, United States sanitary officials prohibited beef shipments because of inadequate sanitary inspection controls. In mid-January, 1915, the villistas obtained the services of a veterinarian to serve as a meat inspector for the slaughterhouse. He inspected meat in Juárez, and, after the product was shipped into El Paso, a United States Department of Agriculture veterinarian reinspected it.[22]

[20] International Land and Livestock Company to Bryan, November 30, 1914; Bryan to Marion Letcher, Consul, Chihuahua City, December 5, 1914, File 611.129/15; Consulate [Leon J. Canova], Chihuahua City, to Bryan, December 28, 1914, File 611.129/18, RG 59, NA.

[21] Hipólito Villa to D. F. Houston, November 5, 1914, Records of the Bureau of Animal Industry, 1910–1939, File 141.55, Record Group 17, National Archives, Washington, D.C. Hereafter cited as RG 17, NA.

[22] Chief, Bureau of Animal Industry, to P. H. Landergin, January 14, 1915, File 312.114P19/2, RG 59, NA.

Villa's packinghouse operation allegedly trafficked in stolen cattle. But George Carothers, formerly United States consul at Torreón and special agent for the Department of State attached to Villa's forces, stated that one of the principal buyers of Mexican meat from Villa was Cudahy and Company; this major firm, he claimed, would not traffic in stolen goods. Most of the meat purchased by Cudahy was contracted for sale through Juárez with Luis Terrazas.[23]

Protests about the slaughterhouse in Juárez came from the Panhandle and Southwestern Stockmen's Association. The group complained that its members had suffered from the seizure of their cattle in Mexico and the subsequent sale of these cattle in the United States. Association representatives also alleged that, although members had been moderately successful in recovering their lost cattle, the villista slaughterhouse rendered identification of butchered stock impossible. Freshly killed beef bore no brand or other identifying mark, and association members with cattle in Mexico were threatened with grievous loss. It was suggested also that the sanitary conditions of such beef probably failed to meet United States specifications.[24]

Such complaints prompted the plant manager at Juárez to invite a delegation from the association to visit the operation and examine its books. The invitation produced no response. Instead the Texas cattlemen dispatched a delegation to Washington, D.C., in an attempt to quash the operation through sanitary restrictions.[25]

Efforts to restrict the flow of villista beef into Texas proved successful. The removal of the USDA meat inspector from his El Paso post paralyzed Villa's operation in Juárez. Villa felt that pressures upon Washington from Texas cattlemen had prompted the move. Carothers urged the secretary of state, Robert Lansing, to

[23] George C. Carothers to Lansing, March 15, 1915, File 312.114P14/5, RG 59, NA. Carothers' contention is supported by letters from Luis Terrazas dated December 21, 1914, in the same file.

[24] C. A. Culbertson to Lansing, January 8, 1915, enclosing a letter from the president of the Stockmen's Association of Amarillo, Texas, and from P. H. Landergin, president of the Panhandle and Southwestern Stockmen's Association, December 29, 1914, File 312.114P19/5, RG 59, NA.

[25] Carothers to Lansing, April 30, 1915, File 312.114P19/6, RG 59, NA.

send objective inspectors to examine Villa's operation. He argued that if this were done it could improve the United States' bargaining position in those areas of Mexico controlled by Villa.[26]

Carothers' intervention failed; on May 17, 1915, the Bureau of Animal Industry (BAI), under orders from the secretary of agriculture, closed the border to meat shipments from Juárez. The secretary's declaration stated, however, that meat from Juárez could be accepted once BAI standards were met. Villa, at the same time, claimed that the packinghouse merely awaited the arrival of a meat inspector in order to reopen and have properly authorized inspection certificates. Carothers again urged a reopening of the port in order to facilitate his own work with Villa.[27]

Villa, in a shrewd ploy, offered to pay the salary of a duly appointed meat inspector. His brother, Hipólito, delivered $600 to Zack Cobb, collector of customs at El Paso, to assure the salary of an inspector for the Juárez plant and to spur the USDA to action.[28]

Department of State intervention yielded positive results for Villa. In late May the secretary of agriculture acceded to demands for an inspection system for Juárez. Mexican meat would be admitted from Villa's packinghouse, provided that inspection was made by a USDA veterinarian and that veterinary assistants would be there at all times. These men would return if they could not bring about compliance with BAI standards. In addition, an extra veterinarian for Juárez required a salary of $200 plus expenses. Funds for the additional salary would be provided from the collection of customs at El Paso.[29]

In early July, however, the USDA again forced the closure of the Juárez plant. Villa, smarting from military reverses, took a more aggressive stand. He informed Carothers that he and his group had made "every effort to give guarantees to the persons and properties of American citizens, resident in Mexico. . . ." Yet villistas saw no "corresponding response in matters we have to take up with them [the Department of State] and we receive no attention, such as in

[26] Carothers to Lansing, May 7, 1915, File 312.114P19/7, RG 59, NA.
[27] Lansing to Carothers, May 19, 1915, File 312.114P19/10; Carothers to Lansing, May 19, 1915, File 312.114P19/11, RG 59, NA.
[28] Carothers to Lansing, May 24, 1915, File 312.114P19/12, RG 59, NA.
[29] Houston to Lansing, May 22, 1915, File 312.114P19/13, RG 59, NA.

the case of the packing plant in Juárez. I would like to know," continued Villa, "if we will be assisted and if our efforts are taken into consideration so as to act accordingly."[30]

Villa's declaration contained a veiled threat against foreign properties in northern Mexico. In early August, Carothers reported that Villa was exerting more pressure on foreigners in Chihuahua. He recommended reopening the Juárez plant in order to alleviate the pressure on Villa; this in turn would decrease the harassment of foreigners in those parts of Mexico under villista control.[31]

While Villa faced periodic closure of his packinghouse operation, he also found himself on the defensive against Carranza. Villa thus became less of a contender for de facto recognition from the United States. Carranza's intransigent attitude, however, forced Secretary of State Robert Lansing to continue to search for an alternative to the Constitutionalist leader. As a result, Lansing requested that a meat inspection station be opened in El Paso so that Villa might sell his livestock in the United States. President Wilson's reaction was one of puzzlement. He asked Lansing if he thought it "wise to put Villa in the way of getting money just at the moment when he is apparently weakest and on the verge of collapse? What will be gained by that if, should he be left alone, he may be eliminated by the force of events?"[32]

Wilson, however, did not override Lansing's attempts to bring about a successful reopening of the Juárez plant. On September 8, 1915, after much haggling between the USDA and the Department of State, meat imports from Juárez were resumed. By order of the secretary of agriculture, a USDA veterinarian would have to be designated by the Chihuahua authorities as the official inspector.[33]

Proposed reopening of the Juárez plant engendered opposition from United States cattlemen as well as from Zack Cobb. Cobb formally protested the packinghouse reopening, arguing that cattle-

[30] Villa to Carothers, July 23, 1915, File 312.114P19/24, RG 59, NA.
[31] Carothers to Lansing, August 3, 1915, File 312.114P19/28, RG 59, NA.
[32] Lansing to Woodrow Wilson, August 6, 1915, File 812.00/15751a; Wilson to Lansing, August 7, 1915, File 812.00/157711½, RG 59, NA.
[33] Mark T. Gilderhus, *Diplomacy and Revolution: United States–Mexican Relations under Wilson and Carranza*, pp. 15–16, 27–29. Lansing to Houston, August 6, 1915, File 312.114P19/28b; Houston to Lansing, September 8, 1915, File 312.114P19/52, RG 59, NA.

men in Mexico were forced to use Villa as their agent or else suffer confiscation of their entire herds. The president of the Cattle Raisers Association of Texas added his protest and asked the government to delay a final decision until the association had met in Fort Worth in September. A major factor that needed consideration was brand inspection, because so many of the cattle sold into the United States were allegedly stolen stock. Villa rapidly responded that his agents would enter into an inspection contract and would personally guarantee the safety of the brand inspector.[34]

Lansing's efforts failed to render sufficient aid to Villa. By September, 1915, villista currency had continued to depreciate, and Villa needed gold to continue his struggle against Carranza. United States recognition of Carranza in October, 1915, forced the removal once again of the Juárez packinghouse from the list of approved agencies shipping meats into the United States from Mexico. Although the ban imposed upon cattle applied also to the importation of bullion, ore, and cotton from rebels, the villistas continued to ship these as well as meats through Juárez and El Paso. El Paso courts attached these goods as contraband but could hold them for only three days once the duties had been paid.[35]

Villa continued his rustling activities and prompted Mexican cattlemen to seek relief through the sale of cattle in the United States. Three companies in Sonora requested permission to ship cattle from Arizona in order to avoid seizure by villistas. Carranza, however, also recognized the value of the cattle and imposed a twenty-peso export tax on the stock. Meanwhile Mexico's Secretariat of Foreign Relations declared that no stock could be exported from Mexico because so much had already been stolen by villistas. It was hoped that prohibiting exportation would put an end to the thievery. Carranza overruled the secretariat, however, and allowed exportation of one herd, provided that the duties were paid.[36]

[34] Cobb to Lansing, August 3, 1915, File 312.114P19/30; J. D. Jackson to Lansing, September 3, 1915; George P. McCabe to Chief, Bureau of Animal Industry, June 9, 1915, File 312.114P19/64, RG 59, NA.
[35] Houston to Lansing, October 20, 1915; File 312.114P19/58, RG 59, NA; Constitutionalist Representative, Washington, D.C., to Mexican Consul, El Paso, October 21, 1915; Mexican Consul, El Paso, to Cobb, October 25, 1915, L.E. 811R, Legajo 4, AHRE.
[36] Consul, Nogales, to Lansing, October 28, 1915, File 611.127/78; John

De facto recognition of Carranza had forced Lansing in October, 1915, to request that the USDA prevent the importation of livestock and livestock products through ports under the control of "any revolutionary faction opposed to the recognized *de facto* government of Mexico, in the states of Sonora and Chihuahua." In early November, the secretary of agriculture pointed out that United States sanitary regulations were designed for the curtailment of livestock disease. "These acts," he wrote, "refer rather to the animal than to the owner or shipper." The USDA did not possess authority to "establish, by regulation or otherwise, a distinction between shippers favorable to Americans and others in Mexico not engaged in the continuance of the Revolution and favorable to those who are so engaged."[37]

Consequently Villa continued his seizures of cattle; in November, 1915, he drove 3,800 head through Fabens, Texas. In addition, he still controlled Palomas, Chihuahua, and thus collected export taxes on all shipments of livestock through that port of entry. The Corralitos Land and Cattle Company found itself forced to pay duty to Villa when it drove its cattle into Columbus, New Mexico. Carranza's agent in El Paso subsequently advised the company that it still owed money to the de facto government.[38]

Villa's continued control of Chihuahua was the despair of Zack Cobb. Despite United States recognition of Carranza, no effective way existed to prevent Villa from exporting livestock into the United States, using El Paso as a major market for the sale of cattle taken from the massive haciendas of Luis Terrazas. In exasperation Cobb declared: "Villa has long since ceased to be a revolutionist. His organization of pirates, manned by Mexican soldiers and captained by American grafters, continues to exist and thrive solely because this port is open to their loot."[39]

Villa's attitude toward the United States soured after its recogni-

---

W. Belt to Lansing, November 2, 1915; John Silliman to Lansing, November 5, 1915, File 611.127/8, RG 59, NA.

[37] Lansing to Houston, October 19, 1915, File 812.00/16612; Cobb to Lansing, October 19, 1915, File 812.00/16520; Houston to Lansing, November 2, 1915, File 812.00/17780, RG 59, NA.

[38] Mexican Consul, El Paso, to Mexican Embassy, Washington, D.C., November 10, 1915, L.E. 811, Legajo 4, AHRE.

[39] Cobb to Lansing, November 10, 1915, File 611.1224/75, RG 59, NA.

tion of Carranza. His forays against United States–owned properties in northern Mexico intensified, and he became less discriminating about the victims of his raids. In December, 1915, he declared expropriated the Babícora Ranch of William Randolph Hearst. The Babícora, one of the larger foreign-owned outfits in Chihuahua, possessed between 20,000 and 60,000 head of cattle. Although Villa's confiscation decree was never implemented, it certainly indicated a change of attitude toward his former friends north of the Rio Grande.[40]

Pancho Villa's growing distrust of the United States reached its climax on March 9, 1916, when his forces raided Columbus, New Mexico. His motives for the raid continue to be disputed, but no doubt exists that the raid was planned well in advance. Two days before his troops struck Columbus, Villa stopped south of that sleepy town and rounded up cattle belonging to the Palomas Land and Cattle Company in order to have a ready supply of provisions when he and his soldiers took flight.[41]

But Villa continued to need money; and so, despite hostility to the Wilson government, he continued to trade with United States citizens. In 1917 and 1918, reports and protests came to the secretary of state about Villa's negotiating with Colonel Charles Hunt (an El Paso cattle dealer and former Arizona politician) for the sale of stolen cattle. In 1918 Hunt secured a permit to pass 2,000 head of cattle and 500 mules into the United States from Mexico, stock allegedly purchased from the villistas.[42]

The difference between banditry by a revolutionary faction out of power and pillaging by a government in power was one of degree rather than of kind. Armed with legalistic paraphernalia, the successive governments in Mexico from 1910 to 1920 seized livestock for military use or extracted exorbitant export taxes in an attempt to discourage the traditional sale of Mexican cattle in the United States. A full year before achieving power, Carranza levied

---

[40] New York *Sun*, December 24, 1915; Lister and Lister, *Chihuahua*, p. 279.

[41] Cobb to Lansing, March 7, 1916, File 812.00/17361, RG 59, NA.

[42] Ramón P. De Negri to Lansing, April 4, 1917, File 812.00/20886; Mexican Consul [Presidio, Texas] to Mexican Embassy, Washington, D.C., September 18, 1918, File 611.127/319, RG 59, NA.

taxes against cattle owned by foreigners. In May, 1913, for example, a British rancher was forced to pay a ransom of $4,480 to Carranza before his cattle could be shipped out of the country. He thus paid $5 per head in an area where no formal export tax on cattle existed at the time. This tax was levied on all foreign cattle raisers in Mexico where Carranza and the constitucionalistas held sway.[43]

In early January, 1914, President Victoriano Huerta learned that revolutionaries were receiving aid from powerful cattlemen in northern Mexico. He began to devise a scheme to confiscate their lands in retaliation for assisting the rebels. "By this means," reported the United States consul in Veracruz, "he hopes to undermine the control of the leaders in the revolutionary movement.[44]

Once in power, Carranza moved more directly against foreign landholders. While he shifted troops from one point to another throughout 1916, during the time that General John J. Pershing's Punitive Expedition was pursuing Villa in northern Mexico, Carranza provisioned his forces with cattle taken from United States–owned ranches in Chihuahua.[45]

United States–owned livestock also proved a convenient source of revenue for Carranza. Late in 1916 his officials passed cattle through El Paso en route to the Mexican consul in Dallas. These cattle, bearing the brands of Luis Terrazas, the Palomas Land and Cattle Company, and the Ojitos Ranch, were shipped in bond for sale at the large livestock market in Fort Worth. The resulting revenue went to the Carranza government.[46]

[43] Ellsworth to Bryan, May 8, 1913, File 812.00/7472, RG 59, NA.

[44] William W. Canada to Bryan, January 8, 1914, File 812.00/10380, RG 59, NA.

[45] Blocker to Lansing, June 20, 1916, File 812.00/18515, RG 59, NA. General John Pershing, recently appointed commander of Fort Bliss, at El Paso, was ordered by President Wilson to pursue and destroy or disperse villista forces in Mexico. The order came on the heels of Villa's daring raid on Columbus, New Mexico, early in the morning of March 9, 1916. The so-called Punitive Expedition involved the United States in further diplomatic tensions with Mexico, especially with Venustiano Carranza. For an excellent study of the Punitive Expedition see Clarence C. Clendenen, The United States and Pancho Villa: A Study in Unconventional Diplomacy.

[46] E. L. Hamilton to Lansing, December 15, 1916, File 611.1224/99, RG 59, NA.

Government sale of confiscated cattle seemed more an act of spite than a systematic attempt to gain revenue. More profitable for the successive regimes in Mexico was the adjustment of export and import restrictions. Because of the export orientation of Mexico's northern cattle industry, it was sometimes necessary to restrict exports in order to regulate the domestic supply of cattle and meat. In 1914 and 1915 the United States purchased $8 million worth of cattle from Mexico. Although this figure dropped to $4 million in 1916, it was apparent that the licit and illicit sale of cattle in the United States continued to be profitable for Mexican cattlemen and revolutionaries—and for Texans.[47]

Juggling of export duties on cattle began early. Carranza announced in February, 1914, that all areas under constitucionalista control would experience an increase in export duties. He levied a tax on calves of 8 pesos per head; on yearling steers, 12 pesos; on steers two years and older, 16 pesos; and on bulls and cows over two years, 20 pesos. According to the El Paso Times of February 15, the constitucionalista debt ceiling had increased to 30 million pesos because of accelerated purchases of arms and ammunition. Carranza needed an additional source of revenue to offset the spiraling indebtedness. Less than a month later he imposed a 40-peso duty on the exportation of single animals. Those shipped in herd lots had a uniform tax of 15 pesos per head levied against them. In mid-October, 1914, with the split between Villa and Carranza already a reality, the latter raised the general export duty on all classes of cattle by 25 to 50 percent.[48]

By controlling the north, and especially Ciudad Juárez, Villa received needed revenues in 1915, through the collection of export duties on cattle shipped into the United States by ranchers in Chihuahua. The villista commander of Ciudad Juárez levied a twelve-dollar tax on cattle owned by the Border Cattle Company in July, 1915, two dollars more than originally agreed to by villistas. In a telegram to the secretary of state, Cobb declared that the "company will pay rather than take chances on faring worse. Matter important as showing bad faith [of] Villa authorities."[49]

[47] New York Sun, May 22, 1917.
[48] López Rosado, Historia y pensamiento económico, I, 142–143.
[49] Cobb to Lansing, July 15, 1915, File 600.127/12, RG 59, NA.

By March, 1917, most United States–owned livestock near the border had been cleared out of Mexico. Only the Palomas Land and Cattle Company continued to run significant herds along the international boundary, and they did so only because of the exorbitant export duty levied by Carranza. Palomas, however, wanted to get its cattle out of Mexico, and Cobb made attempts to bring about State Department intervention. He stated that "it would be a fortunate thing to have theirs [Palomas Land and Cattle Company livestock] imported, so that the border cattle question might thereafter be considered independent of the effect of such consideration upon the cattle interests of Americans."[50] The tax juggling continued through the 1920's with the dual aim of securing revenue for the government and of assuring a continuous supply of meat for the Mexican market.

Depletion of Mexican beef herds during the bloody revolutionary decade produced unprecedented domestic meat shortages and drove meat prices to dizzying heights. Mexican breeders attempted to meet the demand by importing livestock from the United States, but lack of faith in the Mexican currency necessitated payment in gold, which was difficult. In addition, the New York *Sun* reported that cattlemen, in order to ensure safe delivery, were forced to bribe the general commanding the railroad upon which their cattle would arrive.[51]

Mexican cattlemen were divided in their feelings about the Revolution. Haciendas in northern Mexico, particularly in the states of Coahuila and Chihuahua, often became supply depots for revolutionary factions. After the death of Madero in February, 1913, more large landholders became involved in the revolutionary movement, either supporting Huerta or lending aid to his antagonists. As early as April, 1913, the Compañía Agrícola y Ganadera de San Carlos in Coahuila became a rebel headquarters. Hacienda officials, complained Mexico's Secretariat of Foreign Relations, allowed the carrancista brigands to hide their contraband from the United States. This contraband was labeled as ranching equipment and

[50] Cobb to Lansing, March 5, 1917, File 611.127/219, RG 59, NA.
[51] Carothers to Consul General, Mexico City, July 13 to August 8, 1913, File 812.00/8538, RG 59, NA; New York *Sun*, January 11, 1916.

passed through United States inspection into Mexico without questioning.[52]

Supporters of both revolutionaries and huertistas suffered rough times once Carranza was ensconced in power. Foreigners, especially United States citizens, encountered a plethora of bureaucratic difficulties in the consummation of various transactions. The Santa Gertrudis Ranch, for example, was legally purchased, but the carrancista officials refused to record the deed. This ranch had suffered a loss of over $1 million between 1912 and 1916 as a result of cattle depletion. In 1916 it contained cattle numbering about twelve thousand head valued at about $300,000.[53]

Yet the minor dickering with deeds and compensation for losses was as nothing compared with the xenophobic flavor of Carranza's nationalism after his recognition by the United States. Foreigners were widely considered the despoilers of Mexico's national wealth—men who had exploited the country during the long tenure of Porfirio Díaz. Carranza responded to such public sentiment. In mid-August, 1916, the Mexican government decreed that all foreigners acquiring land or rights over mining, petroleum, or agricultural lands (including pastures) would have to verify their claims. A certificate issued by the Secretariat of Foreign Relations was required and was appended, for purposes of verification, to petitions. The petition effectively forced landholders to renounce the protection of their governments in any dispute that might ensue between concessionaires and the Mexican government.[54]

Juridically the most disastrous blow to the Mexican cattle industry was Article 27 of the Constitution of 1917. A powerful impulse for agrarian reform gripped the Constitutional Convention of Querétaro in late 1916 and early 1917, and slashing attacks were made upon the landed estates. During the legislative term of 1918, declared Article 27, "the Congress and State Legislatures shall enact laws, within their respective jurisdictions, for the purpose of

[52] Inspector General of Consulates to Relaciones Exteriores, April 11, 1913, L.E. 762R, Legajo 54, AHRE; Mexican Consul, Del Rio, Texas, to Relaciones Exteriores, June 17, 1914, L.E. 813R, Legajo 3 (1), AHRE.

[53] Thomas P. Fleming to Lansing, April 10, 1916, File 312.114F62; Paul Fleming to Lansing, September 6, 1916, File 312.114F62/3, RG 59, NA.

[54] Oficina de Información, Secretaría de Relaciones Exteriores, to Mexican Consul, El Paso, August 18, 1916, L.E. 806R, Legajo 2, AHRE.

carrying out the division of large landed estates. . . . Each state and territory was to fix the maximum amount of land that could be owned by any individual or corporation. The article continued: "The excess of the area thus fixed shall be subdivided by the owner within the period set by the laws of the respective locality; and these subdivisions shall be offered for sale on such conditions as the respective government shall approve. . . . If the owner shall refuse to make the subdivision, this shall be carried out by the local government, by means of expropriation proceedings."[55]

Article 27 spelled disaster for the cattle industry in northern Mexico. As the early legislatures met, large holdings became special targets for ardent revolutionaries. In Chihuahua, for example, any land that would sustain more than 500 head of cattle was subject to expropriation. As a result, Mexican cattlemen, both foreign and domestic, were loath to rebuild their large estates for extensive and intensive production of beef cattle. Another two decades would pass before the beginnings of an amicable solution appeared.[56]

Revolutionary activities along the border also interrupted the regular sanitary inspection of cattle entering the United States and caused consternation among cattlemen in Texas and the Southwest. Two principal maladies engendered the most concern: fever ticks and foot-and-mouth disease.

As early as 1909, proposals were being made in the United States to construct a fence along parts of the international boundary between Mexico and the United States as a preventive measure for keeping Mexican cattle confined to their territory. The major concern centered upon the indiscriminate deposit of fever ticks by immune Mexican stock and the subsequent infestation of susceptible United States cattle. According to the secretary of agriculture, the Tecate Valley needed fencing. Approximately forty-five miles of fence would be necessary to control those areas where most crossings occurred. Although the secretary of state concurred in this judgment, the interruption of normal diplomatic negotiations by

[55] United States Department of State, "Mexican Constitution of 1917," in *Papers Relating to the Foreign Relations of the United States, 1917*, pp. 955–957.

[56] Charles R. Koch, "Beef below the Border," *Farm Quarterly* 24 (Summer, 1969), p. 48.

the Revolution of 1910 terminated a serious implementation of the matter.[57]

Fear of tick fever and its chronicity in Mexico persisted through the early years of the Revolution. In most border consular districts, the Orozco rebellion of 1912 forced many cattlemen to seek a means of removing their stock from Mexico. The USDA, though sympathetic to the plight of the cattlemen, maintained its strict posture with regard to tick infestation and continued to require that cattle be dipped in arsenical solution before entering the United States.[58] Tick-infested cattle frustrated revolutionaries wishing to sell cattle in the United States, legitimate cattlemen wishing to protect their cattle from seizure by either government or revolutionary factions, and sanitary officials in the United States.

Foot-and-mouth disease, or *fiebre aftosa*, became even more vexatious than fever ticks. Frequent outbreaks of the dread malady in the United States after 1870 had made sanitary officials wary of any reports and probably prompted them to overreact whenever rumors of the disease in Mexico surfaced. In Tampico, for example, when alleged cases of aftosa appeared, the USDA dispatched a veterinarian to the area to investigate. The veterinarian reported that no aftosa existed around Tampico.[59]

Two years later, in 1915, Texas succumbed to an aftosa scare. Frequent crossings of illicit cattle, sold primarily by villistas, prompted Cobb to use foot-and-mouth disease as a pretext to prohibit the entry of villista stock. Texas officials slapped a quarantine on the stock even though the USDA could find no reason to do so. Presumably the conflict among importers, buyers, and sanitary officials resolved itself, for cattle continued to enter Texas after 1915.[60]

Mexico's revolution involved more than a jockeying for power. The total fabric of the nation was torn by conflicting interests and revolutionary factions. As a result of revolutionary activity lives were lost, homes destroyed, and modes of living disrupted. Perhaps

[57] J. Wilson to Knox, April 21, 1910, File 611.1257/3; Knox to Henry Lane Wilson, June 1, 1910. File 611.1257/4, RG 59, NA.

[58] H. L. Wilson to Knox, May 11, 1912, File 611.1257/17, RG 59, NA; H. L. Wilson to Knox, August 20, 1912, File 381, RG 17, NA.

[59] Manuel A. Machado, Jr., "Aftosa and the Mexican–United States Sanitary Convention of 1928," *Agricultural History* 39 (October, 1965), 240–245.

[60] Ibid.

of even greater import was the destruction of some of the modes of subsistence necessary for eventual recovery of the nation.

Mexico's cattle industry was virtually destroyed by the revolutionary process. Beef cattle helped revolutionaries procure negotiable specie for the purchase of ammunition and other war materiel and provided subsistence for the peripatetic armies. Throughout the decade 1910–1920 Mexico's cattle industry was systematically reduced to near extinction. Decreasing numbers of cattle forced successive administrations to restrict the export of beef cattle in an attempt to ensure a sufficient domestic supply. In this no government from Madero to Carranza was wholly successful. A reduced supply of cattle, the issuance of scrip currency, and general political instability resulted in spiraling meat prices throughout Mexico. Consumption of meat came to be limited to those who could afford the price. Thus, dietary deficiencies resulted from unsettled political conditions.

Mexican beef cattle became a focus of diplomatic interchange between Mexico and the United States. Anxious United States buyers along the border saw opportunities to purchase high-quality, low-priced feeder stock that could be fed to market condition and realize a good margin of profit. Cattlemen in the interior of Mexico, on the other hand, feared inordinate competition from massive though irregular influx of Mexican cattle into the Southwest and Texas. Caught in the middle was the United States government.

Woodrow Wilson's attempts to formulate a viable Mexican policy foundered on his own idealism. His continual maneuvering between different revolutionary factions in 1914 and 1915 was reflected in attempts by these groups to sell cattle in the United States. Because Villa controlled most of the major border ports, he virtually dictated the terms for the sale of cattle in the United States by both Mexican and foreign cattlemen. And, although Carranza ultimately won the battle for United States recognition, Villa continued to sell cattle in the United States through a variety of ruses. United States producers with cattle in Mexico needed the outlet to northern markets if their investments were not to be a total loss.

The imposition of sanitary restrictions on the importation of Mexican livestock into the United States also proved to be a misguided attempt to show preferential treatment to one faction or another. Under statutes regulating the import of livestock and livestock products, the secretary of agriculture was constantly faced with the problem of admitting stock belonging to a faction out of favor with Washington. The *ad hoc*, capricious decisions with regard to the packing plant in Juárez proved more effective in slowing imports than did statutory regulation. Sanitation as a diplomatic pawn thus proved ineffectual.

The United States government became further involved in the Mexican cattle imbroglio when it attempted to redress grievances of its citizens with holdings in Mexico. A xenophobic tendency in the Revolution had become apparent early, when revolutionary groups pillaged foreign-owned haciendas and made off with cattle, horses, and other necessities.

Mexico's revolutionary fervor reached its apogee in the Constitution of 1917. A nationalist frenzy aimed at the elimination of foreign economic domination in Mexico. Constitutional strictures against foreign ownership of large tracts of land, especially in states like Chihuahua and Coahuila, made the reconstruction of the beef cattle industry appear unfeasible; Mexican cattlemen, too, felt reluctant to invest in properties that could be expropriated on a seeming whim.

2. An Industry in Limbo, 1920–1934

By 1920, revolutionary turmoil had left Mexico economically devastated. Mexican industries, including agriculture, had declined drastically during the decade of the Revolution, and the nation had had enough of revolutionary reformism. Among those hardest hit was the cattle industry.

Cattle, especially in northern Mexico, played a particularly important role in Mexico's trade with the United States. The industry had developed in response to United States demands for more beef cattle, and by 1910 the Mexican nation possessed 5,142,524 head of cattle, with approximately 1 million head in Chihuahua alone. By 1923, however, the Revolution had taken its toll, for Mexico had only 1,750,305 head of cattle in the entire country, a decrease of 67 percent.[1] Mexico as a supplier of beef on the hoof to the United States suffered severe economic dislocation in the early 1920's; in 1922, for example, Mexican cattlemen exported only 34,096 head, a sharp decline from exports during the period 1900–1910.[2]

Reconstruction of Mexico's cattle industry in the 1920's faced formidable obstacles. First among the principal barriers was the continued though reduced incidence of revolutionary activity, smuggling, and bandit depredations in northern Mexico. Second,

[1] Manuel A. Machado, Jr., "The Mexican Revolution and the Destruction of the Mexican Cattle Industry," *Southwestern Historical Quarterly* 79 (July, 1975), 1–20; Consul General, Mexico City, Report to Department of State, April 30, 1924, Livestock File, Records of the Bureau of Foreign Agricultural Relations, Record Group 166, National Archives, Washington, D.C. Hereafter cited as RG 166, NA.

[2] "El crédito a la ganadería en México," *Revista de economía continental* 2 (January, 1947), 18.

foreign and domestic cattlemen were reluctant to invest large sums of money in the restoration of their operations for fear of expropriation by a government at least theoretically dedicated to the destruction of large landholdings. Third, added to the specific problems of rebuilding a pastoral industry, Mexico and the United States again faced a period of severed diplomatic relations (1920–1923). Consequently, although there were some attempts to restock ranges, it became apparent that cattlemen felt uncomfortable about major investments. Finally, livestock disease slowed resumption of normal cattle operations in northern Mexico because of the area's dependence upon the United States market. Nevertheless, there were signs that genuine efforts were being made for reconstruction; cattle exhibitions and a more favorable attitude by the Mexican government gave hope for the rebuilding of the industry.

Although Mexico after 1920 did not suffer the excesses of revolution that had characterized the previous decade, political instability and its impact on the national economy continued to affect the cattle industry. In 1924, for example, as the rebellion led by Adolfo de la Huerta (interim president in 1920) waned, *de la huertistas* crossed cattle into the United States in order to procure money for the purchase of military ordnance.[3] In 1927, bandit depredations resulted in the death of United States cattlemen in Chihuahua and the rustling of their cattle.[4]

Persistent cattle rustling in northern Mexico forced the Mexican government to appeal to the United States for assistance in stopping the sale of stolen cattle. Mexico's ambassador to the United States, Manuel C. Téllez, hoped that United States customs authorities would prohibit the sale of stolen livestock north of the Rio Grande. The United States Department of State proved cooperative. Because United States cattlemen in Mexico were involved, instructions were passed to Bureau of Animal Industry inspectors at ports of entry to attempt to curb the movement of stolen cattle into the United States.[5]

[3] Mexican Consul, El Paso, to Consul General, San Francisco, April 17, 1924, L.E. 860R, Legajo 3, Archivo Histórico de la Secretaría de Relaciones Exteriores. Hereafter cited as AHRE.

[4] Consul, Ciudad Juárez, to Secretary of State, March 31, 1927, Livestock File, RG 166, NA.

[5] Manuel C. Téllez to Secretary of State, April 12, 1929; J. Reuben Clark

Yet the rustling merely paralleled legal requisition of cattle by Mexican military units. Throughout the 1920's livestock raisers suffered severe losses because military forces engaged in putting down sporadic rebel activity lived off the land and seized livestock for sustenance.[6]

As cattle rustling persisted, the state legislatures of northern Mexico acknowledged the need for action against it. The state of Chihuahua, in its search for legal guidance in preparing legislation, appealed to the Department of State, which in turn requested the states of New Mexico, Arizona, and Texas to supply copies of their livestock statutes. Cooperation was mixed.[7] In April, 1931, Chihuahua passed a rustling law drawn in part from livestock statutes in the United States Southwest. It imposed a penalty of six to ten years' imprisonment for the theft of more than fifteen head of horses, cattle, or mules. Lighter sentences were imposed for lesser thefts.[8]

On top of rebel, military, and bandit pilfering of livestock in northern Mexico, nature contributed to the plight of the cattle industry. Favorable range conditions throughout the 1920's and into the 1930's were sporadic, and in some areas drought reduced the productivity of Mexican pastures. In 1926 drought had not yet reached Chihuahua, whose ranges carried only 100,000 head of cattle, with fewer than 3,000 exported that year. In 1929, however, these ranges too experienced severe drought; the Babícora ranch owned by publisher William Randolph Hearst suffered a loss of over 3,000 head as a result. At the end of 1930, ranges in Chihuahua

---

to Secretary of Agriculture, April 13, 1929; Secretary of Agriculture to Secretary of State, April 24, 1929, File 2.527, Records of the Bureau of Animal Industry, 1910–1939, Record Group 17, National Archives, Washington, D.C. Hereafter cited as RG, 17, NA.

[6] Consul, Chihuahua City, to Secretary of State, July 8, 1929, Livestock File, RG 166, NA.

[7] Consul, Chihuahua City, to Secretary of State, February 18, 1931, File 812.62221/16; State Department to Governors of Arizona, New Mexico, and Texas, February 27, 1931; Governor of Arizona to Secretary of State, March 10, 1931, Papers of the Department of State Relating to the Internal Affairs of Mexico, 1910–1929, File 812.62221/21, Record Group 59, National Archives, Washington, D.C. Hereafter cited as RG 59, NA.

[8] Consul, Ciudad Juárez, to Secretary of State, April 22, 1931, File 812.62221/25, RG 59, NA.

carried 300,000 head of cattle, one-third the number for the period 1900–1910; yet estimates indicated that range conditions had improved sufficiently to support approximately 2.5 million head of well-managed stock annually.[9]

Mexican government officials recognized the necessity of rebuilding the cattle industry. The most obvious need was to increase production for domestic consumption while encouraging the growth of the export industry in the north. Between 1925 and 1928, for example, Mexicans paid import duty on slaughter livestock; however, as a part of governmental encouragement of reconstruction, breeding stock was exempted from import duties.[10] At the same time, the Mexican government sought to discourage the export of Mexican stock until domestic needs had been satisfied. Consequently, cattlemen around Piedras Negras complained about exorbitant freight rates and export duties in the area. They alleged that cattle destined for Ciudad Juárez paid only half the freight rates, or approximately 17 centavos per kilogram.[11]

Export duties on cattle fluctuated radically throughout the 1920's. In September, 1927, for example, duties decreased on livestock destined for the United States; by November, however, the Mexican government had raised the duty to twenty-five pesos per head. The effect on cattle originating in the northern tier of Mexican states was disastrous, for most of this stock eventually arrived at feedlots in the United States. Protests from cattlemen in Chihuahua, Sonora, Coahuila, Nuevo León, and Tamaulipas directed to the Mexican Ministry of Agriculture succeeded in reducing the rate to two pesos per head until May, 1928.[12]

[9] Consul, Chihuahua City, to Secretary of State, March 30, 1927, October 12 and 16, 1929, March 24, 1931; Consul, Ciudad Juárez, to Secretary of State, March 10, 1931, Livestock File, RG 166, NA.

[10] "El ganado vacuno," *Monografías comerciales: Boletin mensual de la dirección rural* 227 (April, 1945), 222.

[11] Consul, Piedras Negras, to Secretary of State, August 18, 1926, Livestock File, RG 166, NA.

[12] Division of Foreign Tariffs to San Francisco District Office, Bureau of Foreign and Domestic Commerce, September 30, 1927, Records of the Bureau of Foreign and Domestic Commerce, File 41.1, Record Group 156, National Archives, Washington, D.C. (hereafter cited as RG 156, NA); Consul, Chihuahua City, to Secretary of State, November 7, 1927, Livestock File, RG 166, NA.

To Mexican protectionism was added the Smoot-Hawley tariff of 1930, which forced a meeting of cattlemen in Mexico City in October, 1930, to protest the economic burden of double taxation. In attendance were many United States citizens who owned ranches in Chihuahua and were equally affected by the law. Faced with a combination of export duties on cattle out of Mexico and United States duties on imports, the industry found itself virtually paralyzed: during July, August, and September of 1930 not one head of stock crossed from northern Mexico to the United States, in contrast to the same period in 1929, when cattle valued at $202,000 had entered the United States.[13] Although range conditions had improved in northern Mexico, the tariff structures in both the United States and Mexico shut off the free flow of trade in livestock.[14]

Export duties, excise taxes, and fluctuating range conditions had their impact, but they failed to depress Mexico's beef cattle industry as profoundly as did the constitutional commitment of the revolutionary government to destroy large landholdings. Based on Article 27 of the Constitution of 1917, revolutionary regimes, beginning haltingly with Alvaro Obregón (1920–1924) through the governments of Plutarco Elías Calles (1924–1928) and his three successors (1929–1934), yielded to pressures for land redistribution and the ultimate destruction of latifundia. The motivation was twofold: first, the Mexican government was pledged to bring about equalization in the landholding patterns of Mexico; second, nationalistic impulses dictated the restoration of the country's landed wealth, much of which was owned by foreign entrepreneurs, to Mexicans. As a result, cattlemen in Mexico, both Mexican and foreign, felt reluctant to reinvest in their devastated ranches. There were some attempts to rebuild the industry, but no large-scale commitment appeared during the 1920's.[15]

Foreign cattlemen and cattle companies became targets of attempts to expropriate lands for distribution. In 1927 the Palomas

---

[13] Consul, Ciudad Juárez, to Secretary of State, October 25, 1930, Livestock File, RG 166, NA.

[14] Consul, Ciudad Juárez, to Secretary of State, January 18, 1932, Livestock File, RG 166, NA.

[15] Long lists of claims against the Mexican government resulting from land seizures can be found in File 812.5200, RG 59, NA.

Land and Cattle Company, one of the largest foreign outfits in Chihuahua, yielded to governmental pressures by selling a southern tract of land to the Mexican government for the purpose of moving "squatters" onto it.[16] Further expropriations occurred in Chihuahua in response to *agrarista* pressures. In April, 1927, El Chaparral Ranch, owned by Anastasio Azcarte, a United States citizen, was threatened with expropriation. In July Azcarte suffered removal of his fences so that his lands could be distributed for *ejidos* (communal lands owned by villages), thus rendering him helpless to protect his cattle. According to Azcarte's attorneys, "It is none other than a damn outrage" that United States citizens should be thus treated in Mexico.[17]

The capriciousness with which state agrarian commissions closed in on foreign cattle companies was demonstrated in the fate of the Corralitos Cattle Company. In May, 1927, the National Agrarian Commission obtained a writ expropriating Corralitos lands for ejidos. Corralitos in turn obtained a writ of *amparo* (injunction) to prevent the action. The National Agrarian Commission, however, ignored the amparo and notified Corralitos that it would take over the property on July 31, 1927.[18]

A major target of agraristas in Chihuahua was the Babícora Ranch of William Randolph Hearst. In 1928, ranch management began to suspect that it would encounter later difficulties when it received a letter from the governor's office of Chihuahua requesting that it comply with Article 27 or be subject to expropriation. The Babícora response typified the plight of most foreign cattle investors in Mexico. According to the company's resident manager, retroactivity could not be applied to Babícora because the company and its stockholders had complied with the Agrarian Codes of 1925. This ranch comprised about 860,000 acres of the state of Chihuahua and was located approximately 175 miles south of the border.

[16] Palomas Land and Cattle Company to Secretary of State, February 17, 1927, File 812.5200/559, RG 59, NA.

[17] James R. Sheffield to Secretary of State, April 27, 1927, File 812.5200/610; Lea, McGrady, Thomason, and Edwards to Department of State, July 11, 1927, File 812.5200/651, RG 59, NA.

[18] Corralitos Cattle Company to Secretary of State, May 25, 1927; Corralitos Cattle Company to National Agrarian Commission, May 25, 1927, File 812.5200/630, RG 59, NA.

Recently enacted agrarian laws in Chihuahua limited holdings to 100,000 acres; Babícora was placed in the position of having to divest itself of about 760,000 acres if it wanted to stay in business. Yet it was obvious that the Babícora titles were legitimate, for the articles of incorporation had been accepted by the Mexican government in 1910, and the company was duly registered under the laws of Mexico in accordance with the Constitution of 1917.[19]

The problem reached Mexico City at the same time that it was being channeled through the Department of State. Ambassador Dwight Morrow, in an interview with President Calles, ascertained that the expropriation order had originated not with the federal government but with state agrarian authorities in Chihuahua. According to Morrow, the order had not been designed as a retaliation against Hearst (who was one of Mexico's least beloved foreigners).[20] On the other hand, Babícora's manager informed the Department of State that the actual orders for expropriation had come from the federal government in retaliation for some of the unfavorable notice that Mexico had received in the Hearst newspapers.[21]

Once news of the possible expropriation became public, petitions for land distribution began to reach agrarian authorities in Chihuahua. Citizens from Temósachic, Chihuahua, for example, petitioned for a portion of the ranch called Las Golondrinas to be distributed as an agricultural colony. In a law adopted in 1922, according to Babícora's manager, such colonies could be established for only two years, beginning in May, 1922. The petition was therefore inapplicable.[22]

As the conflict over the Babícora properties moved into March of 1929, pressures on the Mexican government forced the state of Chihuahua to suspend all action against the hacienda until an inves-

[19] Frank L. Peckham to Secretary of State, February 11, 1928; W. M. Ferris to Secretary of State, February 4, 1928; Dwight Morrow to Secretary of State, February 21, 1928, Files 812.5200 Babícora/1, 4, and 11, respectively, RG 59, NA.

[20] Morrow to Secretary of State, March 27, 1928, File 812.5200 Babícora/7, RG 59, NA.

[21] Secretary of State to Morrow, February 24, 1928, File 812.5200 Babícora/5, RG 59, NA.

[22] Ferris to Secretary of State, March 5, 1928, File 812.5200 Babícora/8, RG 59, NA.

tigation of the circumstances could be completed. Under personal orders from President Calles, the investigation was temporarily dropped; for the time being at least, the Babícora Ranch remained immune.[23]

Pressures against the Babícora Ranch did not, however, cease permanently. In June, 1929, authorities in Chihuahua ordered compliance with the agrarian laws of the state, which mandated subdivision of excess lands for agricultural purposes. Babícora received thirty days' notice to comply with the agrarian statutes. Diplomatic negotiations obtained a temporary reprieve; the matter would have to await the arrival of the president of the board of Babícora Development Company. Chihuahua authorities remained adamant throughout the summer of 1929. Ultimately, the Hearst interest, in compliance with a suggestion from the governor of Chihuahua, opted to divide the properties among members of the board of the corporation and thus technically comply with the agrarian laws of Chihuahua.[24] Even in a period of increasing reform and intensified nationalistic pressure, Mexican officials felt it wise to temper their activities in order to minimize United States reactions against all revolutionary programs.

While agrarian reform and pressures on large landholders hindered livestock redevelopment in Mexico, United States sanitary officials watched warily as a series of contagions affected Mexican cattle. During 1923 bovine tuberculosis, anthrax, tick infestations, scabies, and scours plagued the industry. Scours alone killed 37,850 calves, a massive blow to a nation attempting to rebuild its cattle industry.[25]

Fever ticks prevented the free flow of cattle to the United States and dealt another blow to the export economy of northern Mexico. Elaborate regulations regarding ticks controlled the cattle traffic into the United States. These made no distinction as to the

[23] Morrow to Secretary of State, March 8 and 27, 1928, Files 812.5200 Babícora/8 and 17, respectively, RG 59, NA.
[24] Peckham to Secretary of State, June 24, 1929; Morrow to Secretary of State, June 25, July 3, 1929; Peckham to Secretary of State, July 19, 1929; Consul, Chihuahua City, to Secretary of State, August 6, 1929, Files 812.5200 Babícora/19, 20, 23, 24, and 29, respectively, RG 59, NA.
[25] Consul General to Secretary of State, February 6, 1924, File 611.1259/9, RG 59, NA.

nationality of the shipper; United States cattlemen operating in Mexico were forced to conform to the rules.[26]

Scabies also contributed to restrictions upon the shipment of Mexican cattle into the United States. Again both Mexican and United States owners in Mexico found themselves forced to conform to stringent regulations for the protection of cattle herds in the United States. United States citizens and companies continually pressed the Bureau of Animal Industry for exemptions so that they might avoid seizure of their cattle by Mexican troops, bandits, or both. As with the other infestations, BAI officials were adamant; all shippers were required to dip their cattle before they entered the United States.[27]

One incident occurred that underscores the difference between the two countries in dealing with regulations. In April, 1931, the sanitary inspector at El Paso was presented with a twenty-dollar bill marked "Christmas present." The donor was a Mexican cattleman who wanted to ship his cattle through without inspection. John Mohler, chief of the BAI, was angry that one of his men had been offered a bribe. The inspector at El Paso was ordered to give the cattleman a check for twenty dollars and to tell him that rules were to be obeyed, not suborned.[28]

The sanitary problem that proved most vexing for both Mexico and the United States was the chronic threat of foot-and-mouth disease (*fiebre aftosa*). The United States had suffered from occasional outbreaks since 1870, and as Mexico attempted to rebuild its cattle industry by importing livestock from all over the world, the potential for the introduction of the disease into Mexico was considerable. In 1924 the United States suffered two outbreaks of foot-and-mouth disease, one in California and one in Texas. The Mexican government prohibited the movement into Mexico of United States cattle from afflicted areas until the disease was eradicated. Both the United States and Mexico realized the need for some uni-

[26] Judge Covey C. Thomas to Chief, Bureau of Animal Industry, September 18, 1924; Chief, BAI, to Thomas, September 24, 1924; Thomas to Governor of Texas, September 8, 1924; Chief, BAI, to Thomas, July 22, 1925, File 2.527, RG 17, NA.

[27] An extensive correspondence between the BAI and the Palomas Cattle Company in 1930 and 1931 can be found in File 2.527, RG 17, NA.

[28] Chief, BAI, to Inspector, El Paso, April 9, 1921, File 2.527, RG 17, NA.

form code in order to reduce the chances of aftosa's becoming a permanent presence on both sides of the border.[29] Adding to the necessity was the appearance of aftosa in Mexico in 1926. The far southern state of Tabasco was swept by the disease, and Mexican sanitary officials worked diligently against heavy political and environmental odds to overcome the malady. Both countries were convinced more than ever before of the need for an effective arrangement.[30]

Between 1924 and 1928, Mexico and the United States attempted to reach agreement on livestock import control. Intruding on the negotiations was Mexico's chronic need to import breeding stock in order to build up its depleted resources. Finally, in 1928, the United States and Mexico signed a sanitary convention that called for each signatory not to import cattle from areas where there existed endemic foot-and-mouth disease. In the event that such an importation did occur, the other party could automatically quarantine all stock for sixty days or until it was clear that no foot-and-mouth disease existed. Moreover, should aftosa erupt in either country, mutual assistance would be provided in order to eradicate it. This agreement would lead to massive United States assistance in the 1940's and 1950's in eradicating aftosa in Mexico.[31]

Livestock disease did not deter Mexico from trying to find a way to rebuild her cattle industry. Livestock exhibitions provided opportunities for Mexican cattlemen and agricultural officials to look over breeding stock. Imports from several countries supplemented a stagnant supply of beef cattle for both domestic consumption and resale. In 1922, representatives from breeders' associations in the United States began making overtures to the Mexican government for the preparation of a cattle exposition in 1923. Mexican agricultural specialists examined livestock in Kansas City and Chicago in order to procure the best possible cattle for the showing. The Mexican government agreed to provide free transportation for the cattle, and the railway arranged for the advertising.[32]

[29] Manuel A. Machado, Jr., "*Aftosa* and the Mexican–United States Sanitary Convention of 1928," *Agricultural History* 39 (October, 1965), 240–245.
[30] Ibid.
[31] Ibid.
[32] Consul General to Secretary of State, December 15, 1922, File 812.-607D, RG 59, NA.

Livestock fairs became a major way for the Mexican government to encourage the purchase of breeding stock in Mexico. In 1929, for example, a major fair in Saltillo, Coahuila, served as a means of selling 1,183 bulls valued at $153,434. In early December, 1931, another large livestock exposition was held in Saltillo; its success reinforced this method of obtaining breeding stock.[33]

Mexican imports of cattle, principally from the United States, peaked in 1924 and 1925, reaching 44,597 head and 81,825 head with respective values of 1,505,044 and 3,444,405 pesos.[34] From 1926 until 1934, the number of imports declined markedly as a result of worldwide depression, reaching a low point in 1933 of 2,187 head valued at 254,383 pesos.[35] (See Table 2 in the appendix.)

At first the export of Mexican cattle proved equally sluggish. Between 1916 and 1925 no quotas were fixed on exports of stock from Mexico, nor were there decrees that hindered or favored the cattle industry.[36] In 1924, Mexican cattle exports to the United States totaled 14,354 head valued at 342,151 pesos.[37] These exports reached a high point in 1929, however, when 179,367 head of cattle valued at 7,295,042 pesos crossed into the United States.[38] Even with a worldwide depression affecting both countries, Mexican exports to the United States between 1931 and 1933 reached 67,500 head with a value of 1,378,204 pesos.[39] (See Table 3 in the appendix.)

The statistics reflect government tinkering with export quotas, a general fear of expropriation, and the ravages of economic depression combined with the still depressed state of Mexico's cattle industry. After 1920, cattlemen in Chihuahua, for example, wanted to rebuild, but the Agrarian Code, passed in the state in 1922, limited grazing land to 100,000 acres per person. The Mexican government hoped that in this way more cattlemen would become

---

[33] Press Memorandum, Department of State, December 9, 1931, Livestock File, RG 166, NA.

[34] *Anuario estadístico de comercio exterior*, 1925–1926, p. 1.

[35] *Anuario estadístico*, 1933, pp. 3–4.

[36] Diego G. López Rosado, *Historia y pensamiento económico de México, Agricultura y ganadería: Propiedad de la tierra México*, I, 243–244.

[37] *Anuario estadístico*, 1920–1924, p. 138.

[38] *Anuario estadístico*, 1930, p. 458.

[39] *Anuario estadístico*, 1933, p. 420.

active, but the limitation also served to destroy large haciendas that exceeded the limitation on acreage.[40]

Beginning in 1926, the Mexican government became actively involved in the promotion of agricultural pursuits. On March 10, 1926, the Banco Nacional de Crédito Agrícola was established to render aid to agriculturists. The law was without precedent in Mexico. Monetary aid was given to agriculturists, who were organized into cooperative agencies to assure an efficient use of funds. The Banco was established primarily for the benefit of *ejidatarios* (holders of communally owned village tracts) and small landowners. Larger cattlemen received little aid from this source.[41]

Cattlemen, however, began to organize themselves. In Chihuahua a cattlemen's association was formed in 1926 primarily for protection against cattle thieves. It also functioned as a pressure group for lobbying with the central government in Mexico City; in 1927 it succeeded in prying a decree from the Ministry of Agriculture prohibiting shipment of cattle from Chihuahua except under the regulation of an inspector appointed by the association.[42]

Mexican government officials were not indifferent to the plight of the cattle industry. Within the constraints of agrarian-oriented policies they attempted to encourage the production of livestock throughout the nation. In 1929 President Emilio Portes Gil decreed that the Mexican government should establish nine national stock-raising stations. Eight of these would have agricultural schools, and the ninth would be centered with the National School of Agriculture.[43]

Attempts to change Mexican agriculture required the destruction of the patterns of land use. Luis Terrazas, venerable cattle baron of Chihuahua, provided a major test for Article 27. Additionally, Terrazas symbolized the degeneracy of the ancien régime because of its alleged voracity for land, but Luis Terrazas, con-

---

[40] Florence C. Lister and Robert H. Lister, *Chihuahua: Storehouse of Storms*, p. 284.

[41] Banco Nacional de Crédito Agrícola y Ganadero, *Vienticinco años del Banco Nacional de Crédito Agrícola y Ganadero*, pp. 17–18.

[42] Consul, Chihuahua City, to Secretary of State, March 30, 1927, Livestock File, RG 166, NA.

[43] Consul General to Secretary of State, May 23, 1929, File 812.6222, RG 59, NA.

vinced of the honorableness of men, attempted through legitimate channels to recoup his losses as a result of the Revolution. In February, 1922, a bill introduced into the state legislature of Chihuahua attracted local attention to the vast Terrazas holdings. By the terms of this bill, A. J. McQuatters, a San Francisco investor, and others including a president of an El Paso bank, became eligible to close on an option for the entire Terrazas holdings, which could then be subdivided and resold to Mexicans and foreigners on relatively easy twenty-year terms. The bill exempted the Terrazas holdings from any future land laws passed by the state of Chihuahua. Purchase of Terrazas lands by McQuatters also required his establishment of a private land bank, and an organization called the Compañía Agraria de Chihuahua held the land. A bill of this nature was especially significant at this time, for while the legislature was considering the McQuatters bill it also began deliberations on the passage of an agrarian code for the state, in conformance with the mandate in Article 27 for each state to prepare its agrarian code.[44]

On a broader scale, the federal government began its push for the eventual partitioning of latifundia. Here emerged the conflict: new federal agrarian laws ultimately provided for the seizure of all the Terrazas lands and their distribution to peasants. Several million acres in the state of Chihuahua, carrying an average value of $10 per acre, became susceptible to expropriation. Government purchase of these lands would yield the landholder $1.50 per acre. New landholders in Chihuahua would receive assistance from the National Agrarian Commission, which aimed to establish an agricultural bank in Chihuahua. The government warned other *latifundistas* that they too could be affected.[45]

While two conflicting pieces of legislation received attention in Chihuahua's legislature, Governor Ignacio Enríquez sided with McQuatters and, indirectly, with Luis Terrazas. Enríquez considered the McQuatters bill consistent with revolutionary ideals, for it would parcel out great portions of land, provide compensation

[44] Consul, Chihuahua City, to Secretary of State, February 7, 1922, File 812.52T27/1, RG 59, NA.

[45] Consul, Ciudad Juárez, to Secretary of State, February 9, 1922, File 812.52T27/2, RG 59, NA.

for lost lands, and bring new money into the state, which would speed land division and development. Long-sought ideals would be realized because the new company would operate under the laws of both Mexico and Chihuahua.[46]

At a more personal level, the contract in which McQuatters and his associates agreed to certain conditions became essentially an agreement between McQuatters and Enríquez promoting the economic development of Chihuahua. The Chihuahua State Constitution (Article V) declared that every inhabitant of the state possessed a right to cultivate the soil. By his consent to parceling of the Terrazas estates, McQuatters proved willing to establish a Mexican company for the purpose of fostering a thriving agricultural enterprise in the state. A major complication, however, was that the essentially desert character of Chihuahua soil necessitated the classification of land by the availability of water. Landowners could utilize company forests for lumber and fuel. Under the McQuatters agreement, landowners could not sell grazing lots for more than three dollars per acre. Additionally, when 80 percent of irrigated lands, created from irrigation districts, had been sold the company obligated itself to bring more land under cultivation until such time as 100,000 acres would be cultivated as irrigated land.[47]

The agreement between McQuatters and Enríquez recognized the fundamentally pastoral nature of Chihuahuan agriculture, for 500,000 acres not subject to irrigation was set aside. Of this acreage, no more than 50 percent could be sold in 50,000-acre parcels. This unirrigated land was to be divided into ten zones that at the end of twenty years would be purchased by the state for initial cost plus 25 percent. Experiment stations also were provided for. State workers would staff these stations provided by the Compañía Agraria. Each station would contain 1,200 nonirrigated acres and 500 irrigated acres for agricultural experimentation. Finally, the company committed itself to provide at least ten buildings to the state for public schools.[48]

[46] Consul, Chihuahua City, to Secretary of State, February 10, 1922, File 812.52T27/3, RG 59, NA.

[47] Consul, Chihuahua City, to Secretary of State, February 15, 1922, File 812.52T27/4, RG 59, NA.

[48] Ibid.

Chihuahua, through Governor Enríquez, made some major concessions also. The state agreed to waive all taxes on land when the proposed sales contract involved less than $2,500. In addition, the Chihuahua government promised to secure a federal franchise for the establishment of an agricultural bank capitalized at $125,000. With this capital the company promised to revitalize the cattle industry by importing at least 50,000 head of quality commercial cattle, by establishing breeding farms, or by sponsoring farms aimed at the improvement of cattle quality. Cattle raised on this basis could then be resold in small numbers for the restocking of grazing lands throughout the state.[49]

Unfortunately, national pressures shattered the arrangement between McQuatters *et al.* and the state of Chihuahua, for the legislation that would have enabled such a cooperative deal coincided with the introduction of Chihuahua's agrarian code. McQuatters' bill initially failed to receive even cursory legislative attention. Radical agrarian elements in the legislature, forewarned of the impending bill, forced withdrawal of the legislation until the proposed agrarian law had received approval from the legislature. Agraristas argued that ratification of the contract would place more than half the state's lands in the hands of foreigners. The tabling of the contract rendered it a practically dead issue, for McQuatters publicly declared that his offer would be withdrawn if he were forced to operate under the proposed agrarian code. But Enríquez intervened and answered the agraristas point by point, and the legislature, after reconsideration, voted to review the McQuatters contract.[50]

The United States consul in Chihuahua was exultant about the increased business that approval of the contract would give to United States industry. The McQuatters project would create a demand for all types of commodities produced in the United States: agricultural implements, automotive products, building supplies, breeding livestock, and many other items. The United States consul rightly viewed the production of foodstuffs as a major problem for Chihuahua: food production hung perilously low, and the rejuvena-

---

[49] Ibid.

[50] Consul, Chihuahua City, to Secretary of State, February 17, 1922, File 812.52T27/6, RG 59, NA.

tion of devastated lands had failed to occur. Irrigation, the panacea of desert agriculture, could increase such production. McQuatters and others involved in the disposition of the Terrazas estates could provide competent engineers and thus change the characteristics of the Terrazas lands. It was clear that a lot of money was involved. Although the actual purchase price of the land could not be ascertained, the purchase price and improvements as proposed by Mc-Quatters amounted to $25 million.[51]

Initially the United States consul had reason to sound optimistic. While the legislation remained stalled, favorable articles continued to appear in *El Diario* of Chihuahua City. Sixteen members of the legislature publicly declared their support for the plan; only four openly opposed it. Moreover, McQuatters' willingness to allow Mexicans a 20 percent discount on land promised to ease passage of the contract.[52]

Agraristas, however, remained actively opposed. On April 8, 1922, the legislature suspended consideration of the contract. National Agrarian party members filed formal charges of treason against Enríquez. Enríquez in turn sped to Mexico City in order to gather support by the time the charges were formally preferred. The trip proved fruitless; Obregón decreed the expropriation of all properties belonging to Luis Terrazas that were not under cultivation.[53]

Opportunistically, Enríquez quickly became an advocate of official policy. On April 9, 1922, he announced that the national government strove to prohibit land ownership by foreigners. As a result, the sale of the Terrazas lands would set an undesirable precedent. "From now on," he decreed, "everyone who pretends to sell his lands to foreigners can be very certain that he exposes himself to the same proceedings of expropriation."[54]

[51] Consul, Chihuahua City, to Secretary of State, February 17, 1922; Consul, Chihuahua City, to Secretary of State, February 21, 1922, Files 812.-52T27/6 and 7, respectively, RG 59, NA.
[52] Consul, Chihuahua City, to Secretary of State, February 25, 1922, File 812.52T27/8, RG 59, NA.
[53] Consul, Chihuahua City, to Secretary of State, April 8, 1922, File 812.52T27/12, RG 59, NA.
[54] Consul, Chihuahua City, to Secretary of State, April 10, 1922, File 812.52T27/13, RG 59, NA.

Luis Terrazas and his rather extensive family did not remain passive. They sought redress through the district court, arguing that the lands should not revert to the federal government. The government in turn hoped to allay meddling with its expropriation decrees by claiming that it was attempting to regain lands that might have been illegally ceded to Terrazas by Porfirio Díaz.[55]

The intentions of the federal government became increasingly clear. *El Universal* of Mexico City reported that officials from the Ministry of Agriculture viewed the expropriation as a means of creating small parcels and agricultural colonies. On April 18, 1922, to give further weight to his argument, President Obregón declared the Terrazas lands a public utility valued at $1 million.[56]

By this time, McQuatters found himself short of money. He had expended $50,000 for the initial payment on the purchase price and $120,000 for preliminary engineering work. In the second six months of his negotiations he had paid $100,000 to the Terrazas family and arranged to have the contract extended for an indefinite period. According to McQuatters, the Ministry of Agriculture had become aware of the contract as early as July, 1921, when it was ordered that the official transfer of the lands be recorded. In November, 1921, in order to expedite the sale of the lands, Terrazas had reduced his asking price from $2.50 to $1.50 per acre. On December 10, Obregón had given McQuatters permission to purchase the land. Suddenly, the government changed its mind. For McQuatters the only redemption was the government's offer to return all the money already invested.[57]

Obregón, constantly shifting his position in response to opposing pressures, offered to reimburse Terrazas for lands and legal expenses. But Terrazas' attorneys continued to argue that Obregón had exceeded his authority by expropriating the land. The government rejoined that selling land to foreigners was an illegal trans-

[55] Chargé d'Affaires, Mexico City, to Secretary of State, April 8, 1922, File 812.52T27/12, RG 59, NA.

[56] *El Universal* (Mexico City), April 6, 1922; Consul, Chihuahua City, to Secretary of State, April 18, 1922, File 812.52T27/14, RG 59, NA.

[57] Consul, Chihuahua City, to Secretary of State, April 22, 1922, File 812.52T27/15, RG 59, NA.

action, and that all similar transactions in the future would be treated in the same way.[58]

Serious judicial deliberations about the Terrazas case soon became acrimonious. In Ciudad Juárez a federal judge issued a restraining order against Obregón's decree. The judge also refused a writ of amparo sought by the Terrazas attorneys. Now the case could pass on to the Supreme Court of Appeal. The case failed to reach the Supreme Court in time; on May 13 the district court ruled in favor of the federal government by declaring void the titles on the Hacienda San Miguel. The Terrazas petition for a permanent suspension of action was denied and expropriation nearly complete. On May 31 the Terrazas representative conferred with federal authorities in order to avoid further difficulties.[59]

On June 15, Roberto Pesquiera, the official mediator, announced from El Paso that Terrazas would sell the entire estate to the government, except for a small country home near Chihuahua City, for $1.25 per acre. The government bank would then rent the land to McQuatters for stocking, improvement, and subrenting in small parcels.[60]

McQuatters rightly refused the deal. He argued that the land had been deeded over to him before government intervention. As a result, he forced the government to purchase his investment. On July 11, 1922, McQuatters confirmed the Mexican purchase price: $6.8 million. He would realize slightly less than $1 million over and above his expenses. Four days previously, the government had agreed to pay Terrazas over $7 million, and federal agencies in Chihuahua were ordered to parcel out the lands.[61] Thus, in an effort to satisfy political pressures, the government essentially paid for the land twice. Obregón's action effectively discouraged invest-

[58] Chargé d'Affaires to Secretary of State, April 20, 1922, File 812.52T27/17, RG 59, NA.

[59] Chargé d'Affaires to Secretary of State, May 31, 1922, File 812.52T27/23.

[60] Consul, Chihuahua City, to Secretary of State, July 11, 1922; Chargé d'Affaires to Secretary of State, July 1 and 7, 1922, File 812.52T27/29, RG 59, NA.

[61] Consul, Chihuahua City, to Secretary of State, July 11, 1922; Chargé d'Affaires to Secretary of State, July 1 and 7, 1922, Files 812.52T27/31, 29, and 28, respectively, RG 59, NA.

ment in the redevelopment of the cattle industry in Chihr

Terrazas had become the target of men who desire
He tried to sell his lands to foreigners and collided with ......
cent nationalism, thus earning the opprobrium of liberal and conservative alike. His vast tracts of land and his tremendous power
in activities other than agriculture had, by 1922, firmly established
him, rightly or wrongly, as part of the forces of reaction. His aban-
donment of the nation during the Revolution had wiped out any
memory of his valor against the French sixty years before. Consequently, he became a symbol of the old regime despite his contributions to the nation.

Actions of the Obregón government proved complicated and
ambiguous. On the one hand, Obregón was constitutionally committed to land reform. The Terrazas properties provided an ideal
test for the implementation of Article 27. On the other hand, the
proposed sale of Terrazas lands to a consortium of United States
investors complicated matters. During this period Mexico and the
United States were without formal diplomatic relations. Obregón
attempted to negotiate domestic and diplomatic pressures. Thus,
although the Mexican government ultimately expropriated the Terrazas estates, McQuatters and Terrazas received compensation.
Government officials hoped in this way to lessen domestic and
foreign pressures.

Uncertainty about the cattle industry prevailed among cattlemen, both Mexican and foreign. Mexico's export problems were
exacerbated by sanitary restrictions in the United States. The persistence of unrest in Mexico made the United States uncomfortable
about allowing Mexican cattle to enter for fear that maladies such
as tick fever, scabies, and anthrax might afflict United States cattle
ranges; domestic disorder, reasoned the USDA, would make the
Mexican government less vigilant in disease control and thus threat-
en United States herds.

In the area of foot-and-mouth disease control, both countries
recognized the necessity of protecting themselves against the disease that could destroy an entire industry. At the same time Mexico needed both foreign breeding stock to build up her ranges and
a massive export market in the United States for the sale of northern cattle in order to bring new revenue into the country. There-

fore, although the Sanitary Convention of 1928 restricted Mexico to some degree in the purchase of livestock, it did assure her of an export market in the United States. Only in subsequent decades would the problems inherent in the treaty become obvious.[62]

The 1920's provided an opportunity for United States cattlemen to sell breeding stock to Mexico. Even during a period when no formal diplomatic relations existed between the two countries, commercial relations continued. Cattle from the United States were exhibited in Mexico and subsequently sold there as Mexican cattlemen sought to augment their much reduced enterprises.

Overall, the 1920's in Mexico did not show abundant prospects for a cattle revival. Large ranches had been destroyed in the previous decade. In the 1920's, according to the United States consul in Chihuahua, the operation of the agrarian laws of Mexico aimed at further destruction of large landholdings, making it unlikely that cattlemen would restock their ranges until they had "assurance that they [would] be unmolested by confiscatory laws or depredation by revolutionary troops."[63] It would be another decade before the government and the cattlemen re-established a workable relationship.

[62] For an analysis of the foot-and-mouth disease outbreak in Mexico between 1946 and 1954 see Manuel A. Machado, Jr., *An Industry in Crisis: Mexican–United States Cooperation in the Control of Foot-and-Mouth Disease.*

[63] Consul, Chihuahua City, to Secretary of State, March 30, 1927, Livestock File, RG 166, NA.

3. Bureaucrats, Agrarianism, and Cattle, 1934–1945

By the time Lázaro Cárdenas ascended the presidential throne in December, 1934, the ruling political clique was committed to a redistribution of lands in Mexico. Between 1934 and 1945, Mexico underwent serious economic changes. Political nationalism combined with economic nationalism, and Mexicans attempted to gain greater control over their destinies. Lázaro Cárdenas fulfilled the desires of the Mexican masses to wrest some measure of control from foreign investors and to restore the national patrimony to Mexico itself. In his policies on oil, railroads, and some lands, Cárdenas implemented the economic nationalism embodied in the Constitution of 1917. Within the broad ideological parameters of the Constitution, Cárdenas could successfully maneuver to fulfill revolutionary pledges while at the same time attempting to keep foreign investors in Mexico reasonably secure.

A major area of reform for the Cárdenas regime was the redistribution of lands. Calling into play Article 27 of the Constitution, Cárdenas began a systematic redistribution of lands—public and private—under an ejido system that harkened back to pre-Columbian traditions of land tenure. The ejido, land owned communally by different villages, was an attempt to guarantee an equitable distribution of land and to increase the number of *campesinos* (peasants) involved in market production. Though owned communally by the villages, the lands could be worked either in individual plots or through communal action. Intensification of the ejido program under Cárdenas threatened the existence of the cattle industry in northern Mexico.

Yet the threat of handing out lands to ejidatarios exacerbated the qualms felt by Mexico's cattlemen. These men, some of whom had lived through the turmoil of the Revolution and the uncertainties of the 1920's, remained reluctant to redevelop their large, once productive estates for fear that a capricious government might hand over their replenished lands to incompetent campesinos.

During the 1920's, as livestock disease, United States purchases of Mexican feeder stock, and Mexican purchases of United States breeding cattle caused instability within the industry itself, there remained the Damoclean specter of revolutionary vengeance upon the hacendados who controlled massive tracts of range land in northern Mexico. Remaining cattlemen remembered the fate of Luis Terrazas and the eventual subdivision of his lands by a government committed to land redistribution. They also saw the large Babícora Ranch of publisher William Randolph Hearst, a quixotic, sometimes friend–sometimes enemy of the Mexican Revolution, as a victim of redistribution. A spirit of vendetta seemed to invest the new revolutionary elite.

Although the regime of Alvaro Obregón caused them no massive problems, cattlemen feared that Plutarco Elías Calles, labor radical and alleged Bolshevist, might acquiesce in agrarista pressures and begin massive expropriations. Like his predecessor, Calles engaged in a certain amount of agrarian tokenism, but by 1928 he proved nearly as conservative as Porfirio Díaz.

Calles, however, began to lose his political hold. When the PNR held its convention at Querétaro in 1933, it demanded the institution of reform programs that would ultimately fulfill the promises of the Revolution and of the Constitution of 1917. Equitable distribution of land again became a battle cry. Pressures mounted for an alleviation of land hunger in Mexico. Technologically ignorant peasants, spurred on by opportunistic caciques (bosses), clamored for a just distribution of productive lands and betrayed their ignorance about practical agricultural economics.

The Mexican government, meanwhile, found itself combating a deficit of animal protein. The revolutionary decade had virtually wiped out wholesale cattle production. The Mexican government recognized the necessity of rebuilding the industry in order to supply a nation that suffered from a lack of animal protein. At the same time, if they allowed hacendados to continue their work unencumbered, then liberated groups elevated by the Revolution might well withdraw support from the ruling regime.

Government officials who wanted to reduce the outflow of livestock from Mexico resorted to various devices. The government imposed high export taxes on feeder cattle shipped from the north to the southwestern United States. To make more meat available in Mexico City, it imposed price controls on meat sold from the public slaughterhouse. Throughout the 1920's, the government also sponsored livestock expositions to encourage a redevelopment of the industry.

Mexican cattlemen, both domestic and foreign entrepreneurs, watched with trepidation the twists and turns of governmental livestock policy. Discouraged by official proclamations, they maintained a tight rawhide thong on their purses and allowed their cattle or what remained of them to reproduce on the open ranges of northern Mexico. Agricultural "experts" in Mexico City failed to grasp the complexities of dry land range management in northern Mexico.

Northern cattlemen viewed the election of Cárdenas with grave reservations. Even before Cárdenas was inaugurated as president, state governors and their legislatures began to move against the larger estates. Armed with Article 27 of the Constitution of 1917, they proceeded to make tentative motions toward land redistribution and thereby gave cattlemen fits of apprehension. In Coahuila, for example, the state legislature had swiftly passed a law limiting individual tracts of cattle-grazing lands to 50,000 hectares or approximately 120,000 acres. Although this sounds like an immense amount of land, the arid and mountainous terrain prevented effective utilization of a large percentage of such ranges and would therefore limit the number of cattle produced. Tracts in excess of 50,000 hectares became subject to expropriation and redistribution.[1]

When Cárdenas became president, he seemed at first to be a replica of Calles. Cárdenas entered office with a cabinet handpicked by Calles; in addition, he was taciturn and somewhat colorless.

---

[1] Consul, Saltillo, to Secretary of State, October 21, 1933, Papers of the Department of State Relating to the Internal Affairs of Mexico, 1910–1929, File 812.52/1825, Record Group 59, National Archives, Washington, D.C. Hereafter cited as RG 59, NA.

Yet under the taciturn veneer was an extremely able and shrewd politician who, during the *pro forma* electoral campaign of 1934, built a substantial power base among disaffected campesinos and labor unionists. Within one year Cárdenas proved that he was his own man. He systematically replaced his Calles cabinet with his own, more radical, appointees. For cattlemen, this seemed the kiss of death. Cárdenas had shown his true colors: a reformer intent upon the destruction of landed estates in Mexico.

By late 1935, Cárdenas and his government hinted strongly at a nationwide division of the large estates. The proposed plan was to limit such divisions to cattle-grazing areas and thereby increase the number of landholders in northern Mexico and other pastoral zones. The plan was based on Article 27, which permitted a maximum of approximately 12,000 acres to an individual or corporation. Such governmental machination forced the United States–owned Cananea Cattle Company of Sonora to go to Mexico City to plead the case for all cattlemen. They pointed to the misuse of land by legatees of the National Agrarian Commission and emphasized the disastrous losses and drastic reduction in productivity that could occur when such limitations were imposed. They persuaded Cárdenas to raise the limit to approximately 100,000 acres. At this juncture, however, Cárdenas felt that he had been sufficiently magnanimous and remained adamant.[2]

The half-hearted compromise of late 1935 initiated by the Cananea Cattle Company failed to mollify cattlemen. Some foreign outfits curtailed their activities or even sold out. In late 1936, for example, the Higgenbothem Livestock Company of Dallas, Texas, awaiting what they thought was inevitable expropriation, sold its cattle either in Mexico or in the United States and refused to pay its land tax. Although this was an extreme reaction, genuine concern motivated Mexican cattlemen. They feared that the constant threat of expropriation would reduce investments in cattle and the necessary ranch equipment and thereby keep Mexico in a chronically short supply of cattle. Without some sort of governmental guarantee of noninterference with the cattle industry, it was feared, Mexico could forgo ample supplies of domestic beef and reduce

[2] Consul, Guaymas, to Secretary of State, December 21, 1935, File 812.-62221/37, RG 59, NA.

revenue from export taxes collected on cattle shipped to the United States from northern Mexico.[3]

One United States cattleman in Durango, Raymond Bell, who owned the Hacienda de Atotonilco, received a presidential visit in December, 1936. He was impressed with the reasonableness of Lázaro Cárdenas and with the president's knowledge of the cattle industry. Bell implored cattlemen in Mexico to have patience, for Cárdenas promised that "shortly" a law would pass giving guarantees to Mexico's cattlemen.[4]

The Hacienda de Atotonilco had been a pathway for the "various revolutions and the bandits that followed in their wake." In the 1920's the Hacienda de Atotonilco became the property of Raymond Bell, a man who had had previous livestock interests in Mexico and as a result felt that some restoration could be done on the hacienda. The Hacienda de Atotonilco consisted of two tracts of land: the first, the original *casco* (ranch house or headquarters) of the hacienda, contained 115,000 acres; the second, called the Hacienda de San Juan de Michis, encompassed a smaller area—75,000 acres—and lay 110 miles south of Atotonilco.[5] As Bell began to pour money into the Durango operation, his ranching practices were predicated on efficiency and the production of high-quality livestock.[6]

Bell gradually improved the ruins of a once prosperous hacienda. He fenced the permitted maximum of 500 miles, reduced the size of pastures in order to facilitate livestock handling, introduced the use of supplementary feeds, and purchased carloads of registered Hereford bulls from as far north as Montana. Bell's cow herd began with 3,200 head purchased from the Cananea Cattle Company in 1922 and represented the best that careful genetic selection at the time could produce.[7] Bell was a rarity: when the odds were stacked against cattlemen, Bell had continued to invest and rebuild.

[3] Consul, Durango, to Secretary of State, December 14, 1936, File 812.-62221/39, RG 59, NA.

[4] Ibid.; Raymond Bell, Circular letter to Mexican cattlemen, December 8, 1936; Consul, Durango, to Secretary of State, December 14, 1936, File 812.-62221/39, RG 59, NA; Frank Reeves, *Hacienda de Atotonilco.*

[5] Reeves, *Hacienda de Atotonilco,* pp. 67, 69–72.

[6] Ibid., pp. 6, 68.

[7] Ibid., pp. 73, 74.

Cárdenas proved partially good to his word. In late January, 1937, reports of a federal decree aimed at protection of the cattle industry began circulating through Mexico. According to the consular officials in Guaymas, Sonora, the proposed decree would declare unaffected from expropriation for twenty-five years those lands belonging to one owner that carried 500 beef animals or 300 dairy cattle. There was a catch: immunity would not be granted until agrarian elements had been satisfied through land distribution.[8] On March 6, 1937, the *Diario Oficial* of Mexico City published the decree which supposedly granted protection to the cattle industry,[9] but the sheer ambiguity of the decree left cattlemen suspended in limbo. By the end of the year, Raymond Bell declared that the decree was, for all intents and purposes, worthless; it limited too many things, considering the size of major cattle operations in northern Mexico.[10]

Bell's condemnation of the decree appeared to be mistimed. According to the United States embassy, the cattle industry could breathe easily for at least twenty-five years.[11] In December, 1937, the Cananea Cattle Company had about half of its recently expropriated land restored. In addition, the president decided not to expropriate any more cattle lands in Sonora.[12] In February, 1938, Cárdenas granted unaffected status to a large hacienda in Jalisco.[13] It was clear that Cárdenas recognized the necessity of mollifying Mexican cattlemen: they were a mainstay in the north especially and no government could afford to ignore them completely. Thus, although governments after Obregón gave in to agrarista pressure, successive presidents were also cognizant of the productive capacity of large units of land.

[8] Consul, Guaymas, to Secretary of State, January 29, 1937, File 812.-52/2108, RG 59, NA.

[9] United States Embassy to Secretary of State, March 8, 1936, File 812.52/2128, RG 59, NA.

[10] United States Embassy to Secretary of State, December 28, 1937, File 812.52/2533, RG 59, NA.

[11] *New York Times*, March 7, 1937.

[12] Consul, Guaymas, to Secretary of State, December 3, 1937, File 812.-52/2458, RG 59, NA.

[13] Josephus Daniels to Secretary of State, February 8, 1938, File 812.52/2591, RG 59, NA.

Even eighteen months after Cárdenas' agrarian decree about grazing lands took effect, the response by cattlemen was minimal. In Chihuahua, for example, only nine cattlemen, all of them from large outfits, had applied to the Mixed Agrarian Commission for exemptions. According to the United States consul in Chihuahua City, the small cattlemen seemed likely to be squeezed out of the cattle business. Cumbersome paperwork practically overwhelmed the small ranchers in Chihuahua and kept them from applying for legitimate exemptions.[14] Furthermore, United States cattlemen in Mexico—with already large investments totalling $2.2 million—were reluctant to pour money into a still unstable country. In Chihuahua alone, approximately 10 percent of the cattle land, or 289,847 hectares, had undergone expropriation prior to the Cárdenas decree. Leasing arrangements proved more efficient than outright land ownership. Livestock owners could purchase cattle, pasture them in Mexico for a fee, and let someone else run the risk of government expropriation.[15]

The sheer bulk of litigation growing out of expropriation of large ranch lands served to restrict government action. Any litigation that was initiated dragged on interminably. In 1923, for example, the government of Alvaro Obregón expropriated land belonging to the Palomas Land and Cattle Company in northern Chihuahua. Palomas began a long series of legal maneuvers either to restore the lands to the original owners or else to receive some sort of cash indemnity. The contest was still undecided in January, 1940, when Palomas applied for a writ of amparo to prevent further despoliation of its holdings. In February, Palomas petitioned for recognition of its land rights on those lands already expropriated. Mexico's secretary of agriculture agreed tentatively to recognize these disputed land rights as well as land rights on remaining acreages if Palomas ceased its amparo suit, gave ejido lands to surrounding villages, and divided other lands among Mexicans. The Palomas re-

[14] Consul, Chihuahua City, to Secretary of State, August 11, 1938, Livestock File, Records of the Bureau of Foreign Agricultural Relations, Record Group 166, National Archives, Washington, D.C. Hereafter cited as RG 166, NA.

[15] Consul, Chihuahua City, to Secretary of State, April 18, 1938, Livestock File, RG 166, NA.

action was resoundingly negative. The next year Mexico, the United States, and Britain signed a Claims Convention. Palomas promptly submitted its claim for $4,175,717.21. In 1944, Palomas was informed that its claim was being processed through normal channels; that is, the United States government was acting as the collection agent for claims deemed valid against Mexico. However, Palomas could not claim rights over lands expropriated in 1923, a major point of the litigation.[16] Twenty-one years and seven presidents of Mexico were required to settle the claims of one cattle company.

During the final years of the Palomas litigation and in the middle of World War II, Mexico's government, headed by Cárdenas' successor, Manuel Avila Camacho, attempted to deal with persistent livestock problems. On April 27, 1943, the Ley de Inafectabilidad Agrícola y Ganadera came into being. Some attempt was made to define small property except in the case of cattle. Here the same ambiguity used by Cárdenas prevailed, namely, lands that could effectively graze 500 head of beef animals were considered cattle pastures and therefore not subject to expropriation provided that the agrarian needs of the area had been satisfied.[17] By this time, however, large cattlemen had learned to live with insecurity, and there was less excitement over the law than there had been in response to the Cárdenas decree.

Governmental agrarian policy dictated the need for a share of calf crops produced on lands not susceptible to expropriation. Each state possessed its own devices for procuring calves from cattlemen. Chihuahua required cattlemen to donate 2 percent of their calf crops for the ejidos in the state if they wanted to maintain their range lands intact. Although it was a bitter pill, cattlemen nevertheless acquiesced. To make things worse, however, the ejidatarios decided to leave their calves on the ranges on which the animals had been born, for grazing and watering. Chihuahua cattlemen,

[16] Marte R. Gómez. *La reforma agraria en las filas villistas, años 1913 a 1915 y 1920*, pp. 20–21.

[17] Alfonso Reina Celaya, *La industria de la carne en México*, pp. 145–146; Floyd E. Davis and George J. Dietz, *Beef Cattle in Northern Mexico and Probable Exports to the United States*, p. 19; Agricultural Attaché Report, November 3, 1943, pp. 38, 97, File 812.62221/54, RG 59, NA.

both foreign and domestic, were enraged. In September, 1945, they delivered 830 head of yearlings to ejido communities via the state Department of Agriculture. Considering that the ejidatarios received the calves of someone else's labor as some kind of enforced social conscience, the cattlemen felt no obligation to use their precious range and water to feed animals belonging to others.[18]

In accordance with the Cárdenas commitment to institutionalize society along occupational lines, cattlemen also yielded to government control of agricultural activities. On May 1, 1936, the Ley de Asociaciones Ganaderas took effect. This law divided cattlemen's organizations into three major categories: an *asociación general local*; a *unión regional ganadera*, usually a statewide association; and the *Confederación Nacional Ganadera*. By 1958 there were 1,035 local groupings and 40 regional or state organizations swollen by compulsory membership. At the time of the law's initial passage in 1936, the government felt unready to require membership in what was obviously an attempt to institutionalize the cattle industry.[19]

By August, 1938, Chihuahua already possessed forty-five local associations of livestock growers. Faced with inevitable organization, cattlemen in Mexico's most productive beef state decided to use the associations as an organized lobby for their particular interests. Initially the local groups grew out of the First Regional Congress of Agriculturalists held in February, 1938. The resolutions that gave impetus to the rapid growth of local groups depended on government expenditures. They called for: (1) the establishment of an experimental breeding farm; (2) new, improved methods of registering blooded stock; (3) removal of duties on animals of both sexes; (4) pressure for legislation requiring vaccination against infectious diseases; (5) maintenance of an adequate number of veterinarians throughout the state; (6) rigid enforcement of laws against cattle rustling; and (7) removal of duties on windmills and

[18] Consul, Chihuahua City, to Secretary of State, September 14, 1945, Livestock File, RG 166, NA.
[19] Reina Celaya, *La industria de la carne en México*, pp. 154–155; Emilio Alanís Patiño, "La industria de la carne en México," *Problemas agrícolas e industriales de México* 4 (July–September, 1952), 244–245; Frank Brandenburg, *The Making of Modern Mexico*, pp. 90–95.

barbed wire imported for ranch purposes.[20] The last resolution is
of particular interest; the government, despite a national incapacity
at the time to produce finished products necessary for agricultural
purposes, continued to maintain import duties on these items and
thereby made them expensive for cattlemen and other agriculturalists.

With institutional developments in the cattle industry as well
as in other sectors of Mexico's economic, social, and political fabric,
the next step in the 1930's and 1940's came in attempts to improve
the existing criollo stock. Examples such as that of Raymond Bell
encouraged the introduction of high-quality Herefords and some
Shorthorns for stock upgrading. To produce a multipurpose draft
animal, Zebu cattle were grafted into the native stock.[21] Yet, in a
time of economic depression like the 1930's, the cost of production
remained relatively high; the United States consul in Chihuahua
City reported in mid-1935 that the cost of producing one yearling
in Chihuahua was between $4.17 and $6.94. It was also estimated
that one range bull serviced approximately twenty-five cows per
year for a six-year period. What kept the cost factor from spiraling
upward was the relative cheapness of grazing land. Each cow-calf
unit required approximately 25–30 acres or approximately 12 hectares per head; land in 1935 sold in Chihuahua for around six pesos
per hectare.[22] In the 1940's, Mexican cattle production reached
values of nearly one billion pesos with approximately 56 million
hectares of pasture valued at over one billion pesos.[23]

During the 1940's, demands for beef in the United States increased the dollar flow into northern Mexico. In Chihuahua, for
example, as more beef went to feed the wartime United States,
dollars from these sales allowed cattlemen in the north to purchase
more consumer items and to invest in technological innovations for
their ranches. Dollars also returned to the United States through

[20] Consul, Chihuahua City, to Secretary of State, August 11, 1938, Livestock File, RG 166, NA.
[21] "El ganado vacuno," *Monografías comerciales: Boletín mensual de la
dirección rural* 227 (April, 1945), 207.
[22] Consul, Chihuahua City, to Secretary of State, April 18, 1935, Livestock File, RG 166, NA.
[23] "El crédito a la ganadería en México," *Revista de economía continental*
2 (January, 1947), 17.

the purchase of blooded livestock for breed improvement. In 1942 approximately 60 percent of cattle in Chihuahua were of improved beef type (at least one-half Hereford or Aberdeen Angus).[24]

At the end of World War II it became evident that, despite valiant efforts by cattlemen to improve their product, livestock production had failed to keep pace with other segments of the agrarian economy. In large part this failure could be attributed to a lack of communications, a lack of capital, and a lack of security in rural areas. Moreover, as late as 1946, agrarian reform continued to check rapid redevelopment of the cattle industry. Aggravating the sense of insecurity was a lack of fiscal credit for the cattle industry.[25] Loans for agricultural improvement went principally to ejidos rather than to cattlemen in northern and western Mexico. Private banks, rather than the Banco Nacional de Crédito Agrícola or the Banco Nacional de Crédito Ejidal, continued to supply the bulk of investment capital for the cattle industry during the 1930's and 1940's.[26]

The northern Mexican cattle industry was faced with a dilemma. Although the price of beef cattle increased steadily throughout the 1930's and into the 1940's, much of the consumption of beef occurred in Mexico City, which contained only 9 percent of the population but consumed 37 percent of the cattle sold in Mexico. In the capital Mexican cattle were sold at fixed prices. Per capita consumption reached 23 kilograms annually by 1941 but declined afterward, largely because of increased exports to the United States.[27]

Mexican attempts at breed improvement and export of improved cattle to the United States touched off controversy among cattlemen in the United States Southwest during the 1930's. In the wake of a long series of reciprocal trade agreements between the United States and various other countries in the Western Hemisphere (including Mexico and Canada), increased numbers of cat-

[24] Florence C. Lister and Robert H. Lister, *Chihuahua: Storehouse of Storms*, p. 284; Consul, Chihuahua City, to Secretary of State, April 8, 1942, Livestock File, RG 166, NA.

[25] "El crédito a la ganadería," p. 18.

[26] Ibid., pp. 21–22.

[27] "El ganado vacuno," pp. 209, 214; Annual Economic and Financial Review, Mexico, 1944, Livestock File, RG 166, NA.

tle came into the United States from Mexico. In 1937 the Texas and Southwestern Cattlemen's Association became alarmed and argued that the numbers of cattle coming from Canada and Mexico drove down the price of domestic cattle. As a result, at the annual meeting of the organization, a resolution to the Department of State was drafted, requesting that "the importations of cattle under this agreement [Reciprocal Trade Agreement] be placed on a weekly or monthly quota for 1937 in order to prevent dumping of large numbers on our markets in a short period. . . ." Cattlemen in Washington State followed the Texas lead and decried the "dumping" of cattle from Canada into Washington State. On January 1, 1939, President Franklin Roosevelt reduced the quota of cattle admitted from Canada and Mexico to the United States.[28]

The Roosevelt restriction on imports of cattle from Mexico failed to reduce the number of cattle coming into the United States. Despite punitive taxes of three cents per pound on Mexican cattle exceeding the quarterly allocation of 60,000 head, exports continued to exceed quarterly quotas. Cattlemen, fearful of expropriation, wanted to get their stock out of Mexico as quickly as possible.[29]

While Roosevelt attempted to mollify United States cattlemen, Cárdenas sought to keep Mexican stock at home in order to improve the diet of Mexicans. A new duty schedule was enacted for cattle exported from Mexico. Whereas the earlier export duty had fluctuated between 23 and 28 pesos per head ($4.60 and $5.60), the new rate almost doubled the top figure. The Mexican government imposed a schedule of 49 pesos or $9.80 per head on each animal moved out of Mexico. Because the fear of expropriation remained great, even this exorbitant export tax failed to stop the movement of cattle.[30]

[28] Tad Moses, Assistant Secretary, Texas and Southwestern Cattlemen's Association, to Secretary of State, March 25, 1937; H. T. Bone, U.S. Senator, to Secretary of State, June 12, 1937; Franklin D. Roosevelt to Cordell Hull, February 28, 1939, Files 611.426 Cattle/73, 80, and 105, respectively, RG 59, NA.

[29] Consul, Ciudad Juárez, to Secretary of State, February 20, 1939, File 611.126 Cattle/25, RG 59, NA; *Douglas* (Arizona) *Daily Dispatch*, February 25, 1939, File 611.125/183, RG, 59, NA.

[30] Consul, Ciudad Juárez, to Secretary of State, February 24, 1939, File 611.126 Cattle/27, RG 59, NA.

In apparent retaliation against the Mexican move, the United States began to juggle quota figures on cattle coming from either Canada or Mexico. In 1939, of the 60,000 head allowed to enter the United States per quarter, 86.2 percent would be allowed to come in from Canada, a country that exported few cattle to the United States. Mexico received the short end of the bargain, 13.8 percent.[31]

United States cattlemen in both Mexico and the United States remained ambivalent: those with operations in Mexico felt a real fiscal squeeze; those who sought the restrictions were jubilant. Cattlemen who were dependent upon the Mexican importations asked the Mexican government to file with the Department of State a formal protest at the marked discrimination against Mexican cattle.[32]

The exigencies of wartime changed the United States policy on Mexican cattle. World War II marked a high point in United States cattle production, but production capacity proved finite. Consequently, at the end of 1942, Mexico and the United States negotiated a commercial treaty that provided for a marked reduction in the import tax on Mexican cattle and resulted in 1943 in a 31 percent increase in the number of Mexican cattle in the United States.[33]

The treaty did not, however, take into account the domestic needs of Mexico. In spite of its commitment to sacrifice for the war effort, an upswing in domestic consumer demand for beef forced the Mexican government to declare on June 14, 1943, that retroactive to January 1, 1943, no more than 500,000 head of cattle could be exported to the United States. In December, 1943, Mexico announced that it would continue its restriction of 500,000 head.[34]

The larger economic facts of the cattle industry and the manipulation of export figures did not take into account variables that affected the small farmer and rancher along the border. The long border along the Rio Grande made it impossible to keep Mexican cattle from wandering into the alfalfa fields along the Rio Grande

[31] Consul, Ciudad Juárez, to Secretary of State, March 3, 1939, File 611.-126 Cattle/28, RG 59, NA.

[32] Ibid.

[33] Alanís Patiño, "La industria de la carne," pp. 245–246.

[34] U.S. Department of Agriculture, Office of War Information, July 8, 1943, and January 9, 1944, Agricultural History Branch Files, U.S. Department of Agriculture, Washington, D.C.

valley and subjecting themselves to potential bloat. United States customs officials acted with alacrity and seized the cattle, disposing of them at public auction. In a formal protest to the secretary of state, the Mexican embassy in Washington, D.C., suggested that some informal means of controlling the problem be devised, based on the cooperation of border officials from both countries. Although it was necessary to be ever watchful of potential cattle rustling, too strict an adherence to customs regulations could effect hardships on those small Mexican ranchers along the border whose cattle inadvertently crossed the Rio Grande.[35]

The Mexican government's attempted institutionalization of the cattle industry aimed in part at organization for the purpose of livestock disease control. In cattle-producing states like Durango, Chihuahua, and Sonora, legislation formed cattlemen into organized groups to report the development of infection among cattle in their areas.[36]

Throughout the 1930's and into the 1940's, fever ticks constituted the major livestock health problem facing Mexico. In conjunction with anaplasmosis, a blood disease, the ticks tended to make less acceptable the export beef raised in northern Mexico, for animals themselves relatively immune to tick fever tended to contaminate susceptible animals. Furthermore, as a result of its tenacious grip on the hide of the cattle, the tick ruined the hide as prime leather. More important, the presence of ticks hindered the improvement of Mexican cattle because imported animals used for stock improvement proved highly vulnerable to tick fever.[37] Various northern Mexican states attempted to deal with the tick problem by requiring the arsenical dipping of cattle that moved from one zone to another. The state of Sonora, for example, imposed a fine of

[35] Mexican Embassy to Secretary of State, October 22, 1940; Consul, Ciudad Juárez, to Secretary of State, November 30, 1940, Files 611.12245/23 and 26, respectively, RG 59, NA.

[36] Consul, Durango, to Secretary of State, May 28, 1935, File 812.6222/1, RG 59, NA.

[37] "Las enfermedades de los animales domésticos como factor limitante en la producción pecuaria en México" (Manuscript supplied by the Dirección General de Sanidad Animal, Secretaría de Agricultura y Ganadería, April, 1972).

1,000 pesos on cattlemen who failed to dip their cattle during the dipping season.[38]

Drought in the United States in 1934 forced cattlemen there to seek ranges in northern Mexico for their cattle. A request went to the consul at Piedras Negras in Coahuila to find pastures that were free of ticks, for the tick problem, if aggravated, could delay re-entry of the same cattle into the United States. Similarly, cattle shipped to Monterrey, Nuevo León, for a livestock exposition had to be dipped before they could re-enter the United States.[39]

Interest by the Mexican central authority in the tick problem manifested itself when presidential decrees shifted the tick line from one area to another. Cárdenas also actively encouraged state campaigns for tick eradication. Throughout the 1930's, ticks impeded the progress of the north Mexican cattle industry as an export enterprise.[40]

Anthrax, a deadly livestock disease that also afflicts humans, presented problems in Mexico. Throughout the 1930's the cattle herds of northern Mexico faced recurrent threats and actual outbreaks of anthrax. Inspection systems varied in efficiency. As a result, the recurrence of anthrax, blackleg, scab, and other maladies made cattlemen as well as United States buyers of Mexican cattle apprehensive.[41] In Chihuahua alone, twelve anthrax outbreaks occurred between 1932 and 1937: two in 1932, one each in 1933, 1934, and 1935, five in 1936, and two in mid-1937. The consul at Chihuahua attributed the repeated outbreaks in part to the clandestine shifting of herds in and out of quarantine zones.[42]

---

[38] Consul, Nogales, to Secretary of State, May 19, 1934; Law for the Campaign against Ticks in the State of Sonora, April 28, 1934, *Boletín oficial del estado de Sonora*, May 5, 1934, File 611.1258/1, RG 59, NA.

[39] Consul, Piedras Negras, to Secretary of State, June 6, 1934, File 812.-62221/32; R. G. Tugwell to Secretary of State, July 27, 1935, File 611.125/177, RG 59, NA.

[40] *Diario Oficial*, June 30, 1936, and September 27, 1938, Files 611.1258/2 and 4, respectively, RG 59, NA.

[41] Consul, Piedras Negras, to Secretary of State, September 18, 1934, File 611.1251/56; Consul, Chihuahua City, to Secretary of State, May 28, 1937, File 611.1258/3, RG 59, NA.

[42] Consul, Chihuahua City, to Secretary of State, May 28, 1937, and April 25, 1935, Files 611.1258/3 and 611.1259/36, respectively, RG 59, NA.

Much of the same pattern persisted in Durango throughout 1935, with reinfestations occurring in 1936. Horrifyingly, anthrax spread from Durango south to San Luis Potosí. A quarantine was quickly established, and hides and stock were forced to remain in the area until it was declared clean. In October, 1936, the Durango area was declared clean of anthrax infection.[43]

Throughout most of 1937, anthrax infections appeared in Coahuila, Nuevo León, and Chihuahua. To the dismay of sanitary officials, the malady recurred in Durango in July and was not declared eradicated until November.[44]

Although by 1939 it seemed that anthrax had run its course, the disease surfaced once again in Durango; the last two cases for the year appeared in July. All animals in the afflicted zone received inoculations, and animals and animal products could not move in or out of the infected area.[45]

Blackleg and cattle scab, or mange, were also problems for the cattlemen of northern Mexico. Although vaccination against blackleg was increasing, by 1937 only one-third of the calf crop in Chihuahua had received the vaccine. Cattle scab, like anthrax, presented problems arising from the movement of cattle from unclean areas. Such movement could be attributed partially to laxness by state and federal officials. The United States consul in Chihuahua City reported that local sanitary officials refused to follow up on outbreaks of scab. As a result, "diseased cattle have been removed from infected zones in open violation of quarantine regulations."[46]

Inspection of livestock by federal authorities was usually limited to cattle being shipped by rail. The largest single cause of outbreaks of anthrax, blackleg, and scab, however, was the intrastate

[43] Consul, Durango, to Secretary of State, July 11, September 7, December 5, 1935, July 8, October 23, 1936; Consul, San Luis Potosí, to Secretary of State, September 18, 1935, Files 611.1251/58, 59, 61, 62, 64, and 60, respectively, RG 59, NA.

[44] Consul, Piedras Negras, to Secretary of State, July 8, July 6, 1937; Consul, Monterrey, to Secretary of State, October 23 and 29, 1936; Consul, Durango, to Secretary of State, July 9 and November 24, 1937, Files 611.1251/66, 68, 63, 64, 67, 69, respectively, RG 59, NA.

[45] Consul, Durango, to Secretary of State, August 7, 1939, File 611.1251/70, RG 59, NA.

[46] Consul, Chihuahua City, to Secretary of State, May 28, 1937, File 611.1258/3, RG 59, NA.

movement of cattle. Municipal authorities ultimately proved ineffectual in controlling the outbreaks of cattle diseases.[47]

In response to the obvious threat of livestock disease, the Bureau of Animal Industry decreed on December 16, 1938, that all cattle, before being allowed entry to the United States, would require a health certificate. In addition, cattle originating in tick areas were required by law to be dipped. Tuberculin tests and Bang's tests were also mandated. Furthermore, dairy and breeding cattle exported to Mexico needed a tuberculin test before they were allowed to cross south of the Rio Grande.[48]

The presence of foot-and-mouth disease in Mexico and the United States in the 1920's led both nations to conclude a sanitary convention in 1930. As a result, Mexico, bound by treaty, could not help Argentina in a time of economic desperation. Argentina lost her traditional European markets and at the same time suffered from endemic foot-and-mouth disease. She sought outlets for her meat products—hams, in the case of Mexico—in the Western Hemisphere. But the United States and Mexican markets were closed to Argentine imports.[49]

Resilience and tenacity characterized the cattle industry during the Cárdenas regime. Despite constant meddling by the government, despite pressures from agraristas covetous of cattle lands, and despite governmental accommodation of peasant demands, the cattle industry survived the government, weather, disease, and economic depression. Too much assertiveness on the part of cattlemen drew too much attention from agrarian elements and from a government attuned to the revolutionary credo.

Cattlemen were forced to adapt in order to survive. Perhaps the legacy of their frontier beginnings allowed them to bounce back. Mexico's cattle industry, much like that in the United States, was an integral part of a developing frontier tradition of individual dominance and high-risk activity. In the 1930's, the high risks were

[47] Ibid.

[48] BAI Order 368, Regulations Concerning the Inspection and Quarantine of Livestock Imported or Exported into Mexico, December 16, 1938, Effective January 16, 1939, File 611.125/181, RG 59, NA.

[49] Josephus Daniels to Secretary of State, January 31, 1941, File 612005/22, RG 59, NA. See also Manuel A. Machado, Jr., *AFTOSA: Foot-and-Mouth Disease and Inter-American Relations.*

no longer cattle rustlers or rapacious revolutionary and government troops, but rather ideologically and politically motivated officials who hoped to extinguish the traditional cattle industry because it represented some sore of fragmentary tie with the old regime. Juggling of export taxes and the diplomatic complications caused by Mexico's attempt to rebuild her cattle industry further impeded the labors of Mexican cattlemen. Even combating livestock disease became subject to bureaucratic control and to its attendant general laxness. But Cárdenas also paved the way for some relief for the cattle industry. *Tata* Lázaro, as he was fondly known by the campesinos, recognized the differences among Mexico's regions and the economic realities of the north even while he attempted to homogenize agriculture.[50] Thus, although Cárdenas was restricted by revolutionary commitment in his assistance to the last remnants of the old regime, he aided the cattle industry through a decree of unaffectability and the formation of the Confederación Nacional Ganadera.

[50] Brandenburg, *Modern Mexico*, p. 97.

4. An Industry Embattled: Foot-and-Mouth Disease in Mexico, 1946–1954

SUCCESSFUL prosecution of the war against the Axis powers by the Allies transformed relations between the United States and Latin America. Throughout the war Latin America had made significant sacrifices for the war effort, altering development plans in order to supply raw materials for United States production. The end of the war brought with it economic dislocation and placed a strain on United States–Latin American relations. In Mexico, men and materials had helped fuel the war machine in the United States, and diplomatic gurus in Washington attempted to find minor ways to placate a chronically suspicious government in Mexico City.

During the 1930's and 1940's both Mexico and the United States had repeatedly violated the Sanitary Convention of 1928. Mutual effort in disease control was compromised, however; in October, 1945, Mexico, apparently with United States blessing, imported 120 Zebu bulls from Brazil with no retaliatory embargo. One Texas breeder also brought in Zebus via Mexico without a reported word of complaint from his government.[1] Texas breeders apparently planned to sell their Zebus as breeding stock to Mexicans and other North Americans, thus creating a serious problem for both countries, for Mexico chose to purchase its stock directly from

---

[1] For a detailed study of Mexican–United States cooperation in aftosa control see Manuel A. Machado, Jr., *An Industry in Crisis: Mexican–United States Cooperation in the Control of Foot-and-Mouth Disease*; Guillermo Quesada Bravo, *La verdad sobre el ganado cebú brasileño, la fiebre aftosa y la cuarentena en la Isla de Sacrificios*, pp. 13–15, 49–50; Mervin G. Smith, "The Mexican Beef Cattle Industry," *Foreign Agriculture* 19 (November, 1944), 254; *Agriculture in the Americas* 4 (September, 1944), p. 162; and James A. Porter, *Doctor, Spare My Cow*, p. viii. All these sources provide detailed information on the beginnings of the schism about the Brazilian bulls.

Brazil. According to Mexican Secretary of Agriculture Marte R. Gómez, Brazil again attempted to export Zebu bulls to Mexico in 1946, but at this point Gómez refused permission for the entry of the animals. Pressure was brought to bear on Gómez by President Manuel Avila Camacho, and the secretary relented to the extent of allowing the landing of 327 Zebus on Isla de Sacrificios, off the cost of Veracruz, for precautionary inspection and quarantine.[2]

When the cattle arrived, they were quarantined aboard ship because Gómez had ordered a series of tests meant to safeguard his country from a possible epidemic of foot-and-mouth disease. At the same time, the United States, in an about-face, took radical action and embargoed all Mexican stock entering the United States. The blow to the economy of northern Mexico was catastrophic. During World War II and in the year following, Mexican cattlemen had sold as many as 500,000 head of cattle annually to the United States; the newly imposed embargo eliminated this lucrative market. Throughout the summer of 1946 Mexico attempted to negotiate repeal of the embargo. Both Foreign Relations Secretary Francisco Castillo Nájera and the United States–Mexican Mixed Agricultural Commission failed. If Mexico wanted the embargo lifted, she would have to rid herself of the bulls. The United States, however, agreed to a series of observations and tests by a team of veterinarians drawn from both countries. If these proved negative, the quarantine might be lifted.[3]

Investigations began as soon as the bulls debarked on August 31; after a long series of tests, they were considered free of evidence of contagion. Gómez reported, however, that he maintained a skeptical attitude and ordered that the animals "remain completely localized and isolated, with no contact with other cattle than those placed as detectors in the observation pastures." The animals were finally landed on the mainland on September 24, and President Harry S Truman lifted the embargo on Mexican stock. Gómez, however, refused to yield to the "deceitful exhilaration" that pre-

[2] Marte R. Gómez, "The Truth about the Brahmans: Speculations on Foot-and-Mouth Disease," 1947, [Third] California *Senate Report*, pp. 102–103.

[3] Gómez, "Truth," 1947, [Third] California *Senate Report*, especially pp. 112–113, 114, 121, 124–130, 134, 138–140, 148–150; *Excelsior* (Mexico City), June 3, 1946; R. E. Seltzer and T. M. Stubblefield, *Marketing Mexican Cattle in the United States*.

vailed, and warned that any movement of the bulls would result in stiff fines.[4]

The Zebu bulls caused a furor in Mexico. Gómez accused Guillermo Quesada Bravo, former director of husbandry, of acting as the agent for Brazilians who hoped to use Mexico as a way station for selling their stock to Texas breeders. Quesada Bravo, on the other hand, alleged that Gómez, in an attempt to conceal his own complicity in the matter, had used political character assassination to destroy his career. Mexican newspapers and the cattlemen's uniones regionales ganaderas soon became extremely partisan, and vitriolic polemics covered the pages of Mexico City journals. Ultimately Gómez won; he was staunchly supported by the cattlemen's associations and had at his disposal the resources of the government.[5]

In December, 1946, a new regime came into power, and Miguel Alemán Valdéz, the new president, appointed Narzario S. Ortiz Garza as Gómez' successor. Gómez, in a brief to Ortiz Garza, outlined the difficulties encountered with the bulls and the potential danger of foot-and-mouth disease. He wrote, "The danger of foot-and-mouth disease is real, and in case of erring, better through excess of caution than for lack of it."[6]

The United States ostensibly remained aloof from the political wrangling between Gómez and Quesada Bravo in Mexico, though it might be judged culpable for its lack of official firmness about the bulls. By this time United States relations in Latin America began to show signs of strain, and it was hoped that the tacit modification of quarantine restrictions on the Brazilian Zebus would improve the United States' position with Brazil. Brazilian public opinion, based on newspaper reports, coincided with official Brazilian government judgment about sanitary requirements at the time;

[4] Gómez, "Truth," 1947, [Third] California Senate Report, pp. 150, 160–161, 164–165; "Joint Mexican–United States Veterinary Commission Report in Relation to Cattle Imported from Brazil," October 16, 1946, [First] California Senate Report, pp. 327–328; Dallas Morning News, quoted in [First] California Senate Report, p. 346.

[5] Gómez, "Truth," 1947, [Third] California Senate Report; Quesada Bravo, La verdad; also see El Universal (Mexico City), June 18, 20, and 22, 1946; and Excelsior, August 30, September 1 and 3, 1946.

[6] Gómez, "Truth," 1947, [Third] California Senate Report, pp. 166–167.

the possible alternative of dumping the bulls into the Gulf of Mexico promised additional strain on United States–Brazilian relations.

La fiebre aftosa soon struck Mexico; by late October, 1946, the Port of Veracruz, where the bulls had debarked, was infected. Within less than a month the *municipio* (county) of Boca del Río, Veracruz, reported 300 head of infected cattle.[7] Confusion reigned as the disease spread. According to Dr. Fernando Camargo Núñez, many cattle raisers mistook the disease for vesicular stomatitis, or *mal de la yerba*. Preliminary diagnosis of foot-and-mouth disease by Camargo and José Figueroa, buttressed by diagnoses by USDA veterinarians, led to official declaration of aftosa in Mexico on December 26. The United States closed its borders to Mexican livestock and livestock products. Large, alarming headlines announced the closure of the border, and foot-and-mouth disease pushed relentlessly into the Federal District and the states of Veracruz, México, Tlaxcala, and Puebla. Within a month, the infected zone comprised seventeen states, including 57 million hectares of Mexico's agricultural land and 15 million cattle, hogs, sheep, and goats. The movement of campesinos over the hills and mountains with little, if any, regard for a quarantine that they did not understand, intensified the problem.[8] By mid-January, 1947, there were at least 35,000 head of infected cattle in Mexico; yet Ortiz Garza stated optimistically that the "crisis could be considered past if taken into account that there exist in Mexico ten million head of cattle."[9] The disease, however, continued to spread.

[7] Statement of Paul J. Revely, Acting Chief, Division of Mexican Affairs, U.S. Department of State, *Eradication of Foot-and-Mouth Disease. Hearings Before a Subcommittee of the Committee on Agriculture*, House of Representatives, 80th Congress, First Session, December 3, 4, and 5, 1947, p. 143. Hereafter cited as House Hearings.

[8] Oscar Flores, "Remarks to the California Senate," March 9, 1950, [Third] California *Senate Report*, p. 33; USDA, "Foot-and-Mouth Disease," *Farmers' Bulletin No. 666*, pp. 4–5; Federico Rubio Lozano *et al.* to the Mixed Mexican–United States Agricultural Commission, January 24, 1947, private archives of Dr. Fernando Camargo Núñez, Mexico City (hereafter cited as Camargo Archives). Comisión contra la Fiebre Aftosa, *La fiebre aftosa en México*, pp. 4, 11, 15; interview with Dr. Fernando Camargo Núñez, Mexico City, June 25, 1962; *El Universal*, December 30, 1946, provides a good example of the newspaper coverage given to the closure of the border to Mexican stock.

[9] *El Universal*, January 10, 1947.

The Mexican government began its operations against aftosa with very little technical experience. The most efficient methods of eradication known at the time were inspection, slaughter of infected and exposed stock, deep burial, and rigid disinfection and quarantine, known in Mexico as the Alemán–Ortiz Garza plan.[10] Although one critic blamed the slowness of the Mexican bureaucracy for the rapid spread of the disease, a National Commission to Combat Aftosa was formed in January, 1947, and it undertook the drastic eradication measures called for in the Alemán–Ortiz Garza plan.[11] The Mexican Army provided quarantine stations, transportation, and police control for the sanitary brigades, and local *juntas municipales* (municipal directorates) and regional cattlemen's organizations in the affected areas gave immediate promises of support to the National Commission.[12]

To the Mexican campesino, aftosa was an almost unknown phenomenon; officials and technicians groped for a means of making the campesino understand the necessity of severe measures in order to eradicate the disease. The state committees and the juntas municipales joined the director of husbandry, Dr. José Figueroa, in the distribution of over 200,000 propaganda items. United States involvement began at the same time with the closure of the border in December, 1946, and Dr. Fernando Camargo flew to Washington with Oscar Flores, undersecretary of animal husbandry, to negotiate for United States aid. Cooperation became inter-American when United States, Chilean, Brazilian, and Argentine scientists

[10] Lozano *et al.* to the Animal Industry Subcommission of the Mexican–United States Agricultural Commission, January 8, 1947, Miscellaneous Papers, Library of the Dirección General de Investigaciones Pecuarias (hereafter cited as Lozano *et al.*); open letter from Oscar Flores in *Excelsior*, October 25, 1947; Camargo interview; Ramón Auró Saldaña, *Factores que han influído en la extensión y la propagación de la fiebre aftosa en nuestro país*, p. 22; Comisión, *Fiebre aftosa*, pp. 15, 22, 27.

[11] General Order, Comandancia Militar de la Campaña contra la Fiebre Aftosa, Estado Mayor, March 15, 1947, Miscellaneous Papers, Palo Alto Library, Palo Alto, D.F.

[12] See issues of *Excelsior*, *El Universal*, and *Ultimas Noticias* (Mexico City) for the first six months of 1947 for details on the formation of the juntas municipales and the state committees.

joined Mexico in its attempts to rid itself of foot-and-mouth disease.[13]

United States cattlemen favored aid to Mexico because the threat of aftosa presented an immediate danger to their own interests. Congress rushed through a bill authorizing the secretary of agriculture to give aid to Mexico in order to protect vital United States interests. On March 1, President Truman signed the bill into law, and the USDA, along with the State Department and the Secretariat of Foreign Relations, began developing a program for aid to Mexico. On March 6 the Mexican–United States Agricultural Commission met and agreed on a mutually acceptable program. Their recommendations included the creation of a joint commission based in Mexico City with a Mexican director and a United States codirector, each section of the commission to be composed of three members from each country and an unlimited number of advisors. Compensation for slaughtered stock was divided between the two countries; the United States was to pay for cattle (*ganado mayor*), Mexico for sheep, goats, and hogs (*ganado menor*). Veterinarians of the two nations worked side by side. Mexico supplied the laborers; the United States provided most of the technicians and equipment. The Mexican military was given complete police power to enforce Commission requirements. On March 18, 1947, an agreement between Mexico and the United States established financial, administrative, and procedural ground rules, and on April 1 the Comisión México–Americana para la Eradicación de la Fiebre Aftosa (CMAPEFA) began to function.[14]

CMAPEFA vigorously entered the fray under the direction of

[13] Comisión, *Fiebre aftosa*, pp. 16, 22, 27; Camargo interview; *El Universal*, January 5, 9, and 11, 1947.

[14] *Congressional Record*, 80th Congress, First Session; see the proceedings of both houses from January through May of this session, and specifically the *Record* of February 21, 1947; *El Universal*, February 25, March 1, 7, and 30, 1947; John A. Hopkins, "Fight against Hoof-and-Mouth Disease in Mexico," *Agriculture in the Americas* 7 (June–July, 1947), 96; American Broadcasting Company interview with Don Stoops, USDA attaché, United States Embassy, Mexico City, April 5, 1947, Camargo Archives; Comisión, *Fiebre aftosa*, p. 15; U.S. Department of State, *Treaties and other International Acts, Series No. 2404; Eradication of Foot-and-Mouth Disease in Mexico*, pp. 6–8; USDA, Agricultural Research Administration, Press Release, March 11, 1947, [First] California *Senate Report*, p. 383. Hereafter cited as USDA, ARA.

Oscar Flores and Dr. Maurice S. Shahan of the BAI. Flores remained as director until the end of the campaign in 1954, but the United States changed its codirectors twice, appointing General Harry H. Johnson in 1948 and replacing him with Dr. Leroy R. Noyes after May, 1951. Mexico was divided into "infected," "buffer," and "clean" zones, and all animal transportation became subject to strict quarantine regulations under the direction of commission veterinarians. Animals within an infected zone could not move to other regions, and products of livestock in the afflicted areas were refused transport out of the zone.[15]

Aftosa seriously disrupted Mexico's economy and society. The United States allowed the border to remain open to tourist traffic and nonlivestock commerce in an attempt to ameliorate the economic dislocation that aftosa had imposed on Mexico; nevertheless, cattle producers, especially those in Sonora, Chihuahua, and Coahuila, suffered severely. The three states lost an annual export potential of 304,793 head of cattle valued at 32,417,365 pesos. In addition, the slaughter operations undercut both rural and urban meat and milk supplies. Shysters and prostitutes quickly separated the campesino from the money he received in compensation for his stock. Finally, eradication measures rapidly reduced the supply of oxen, the principal work animals, and thus brought about a serious corn crop failure in the first year of the campaign.[16] In less than a year CMAPEFA, despite opposition by the United States, was forced to change from an all-out slaughter program, the only sure method of eradication, to an unproven modified slaughter-vaccine approach in an attempt to save the rural economy.

Equitable compensation proved a problem for CMAPEFA; even before the creation of that body the National Commission had

[15] Hopkins, "Hoof-and-Mouth Disease," p. 96; USDA, "Foot-and-Mouth Disease," *Farmers' Bulletin No. 666*, p. 10; Dirección General de Ganadería, Reglamento, May 8, 1947, Miscellaneous Papers, Palo Alto Library. All these spell out in detail the restrictions on livestock movement.

[16] *Excelsior*, February 14, 1947; Comisión, *Fiebre aftosa*, pp. 15–16; *El Universal*, January 2, 1947; American Broadcasting Company Interview with Oscar Flores, April 5, 1947, Camargo Archives; Statement of B. T. Simms, BAI Director, *House Hearings*, p. 2; Camargo interview; Statement of General Charles H. Corlett, Retired, Special Representative of the Secretary of Agriculture, *House Hearings*, p. 29.

found itself without sufficient funds for adequately compensating livestock raisers.[17] Minimum standards were established, but bureaucratic snarls hindered efficient operation. Finally joint handling of funds was decided upon, with the United States paying the bulk of the compensations. Along with the monetary compensation given the peasants, the USDA and ranchers in northern Mexico, not yet stricken with aftosa, supplied tractors, horses, and mules to the infected regions for use as draft stock.[18] The peasants, however, failed to appreciate the mules and their idiosyncracies:

They learned that the mule was an animal without patience. Beat him and curse him, and the beast fought back. He kicked and he bit. He took fright at all manner of foolish things and wrecked harnesses and plows. And even when he was willing to follow the furrow, he walked too fast.

Ay! How one did pant, trying to keep up with the seedless beasts! How the sweat did pour! How one's legs did ache! How one did long for the slow, patient gait of the oxen—the gait of Mexico.[19]

Cattle that remained in the infected region but were not directly exposed to foot-and-mouth disease presented another problem. Such cattle could not be moved nor could their milk be shipped. As a result, Mexico City suffered milk shortages. One solution was the movement of cattle into central Mexico in an attempt to allay a critical situation. Salvage operations, or using animals in the infected zone, also began, though they were criticized by both the United States Congress and Mexico City newspapers.[20] These efforts failed to relieve a meat shortage in the afflicted zone; and San Luis Potosí, for example, complained of shortages because of the amount of paperwork required to move livestock to market.[21]

[17] *Novedades* (Mexico City), January 3, 1948.

[18] Lozano *et al.* to Subcommission of the Mexican–United States Mixed Agricultural Commission, January 24, 1947, Camargo Archives; Minutes of CMAPEFA Meeting, May 6 and 7, July 30, 1947. Camargo Archives; Simms Statement, *House Hearings*, pp. 15, 18; *Excelsior*, October 13, 1947.

[19] Fred Gipson and Bill Leftwich, The *"Cow Killers": With the Aftosa Commission in Mexico*, p. 33.

[20] *El Universal*, January 6, 1947; Minutes of CMAPEFA Meeting, May 6 and 7, July 30, 1947, Camargo Archives; *Excelsior*, October 13, 22, and 28, 1947; *House Hearings*, p. 89.

[21] *Novedades*, January 10, 1948.

Salvage operations in the infected and buffer zones failed to avert the potential ruin of northern Mexico. The cattle glut in the northern states led to plans in December, 1947, for cannery construction in the north. By this means, potentially infected meat could be rendered safe. Although the prices paid for the canned meat were only about half those formerly received in the United States, *norteño* cattlemen preferred those prices to ruin. In 1948 the USDA negotiated contracts for 73 million pounds of canned meat. By 1951 the United States had purchased 218 million pounds of canned meat, 150 million pounds of which were sold to European countries. Moreover, in 1949 the USDA noted that Mexico's inspection service had so improved that salt-cured meat was allowed entry, under rigorous supervision. These cooperative efforts removed the stigma from the closed border, which no longer symbolized Yankee stubbornness.[22]

During the initial phases of the joint operation, CMAPEFA faced supply problems such as lack of heavy machinery for digging burial fossas, tractors, and laboratory equipment. Much of this essential material soon came from the United States.[23] As the campaign developed, additional storage facilities were needed, and warehouse construction began at San Jacinto in the Federal District, the headquarters of the Dirección General de Investigaciones Pecuarias (General Directorate of Agricultural Research), and in provincial areas such as Zacatecas, San Luis Potosí, and Guadalajara.[24]

President Miguel Alemán contributed personally to the campaign against foot-and-mouth disease. On June 6, 7, and 8, 1947, he traveled through the states of Querétaro, México, and Guanajuato to gain personal support for the eradication measures undertaken by CMAPEFA.[25] In the main, his trip proved a success, although

[22] Statement of Charles W. Wiswell, *House Hearings*, pp. 61–63; USDA, ARA, Press Release, March 18, 1948, [Second] California *Senate Report*, p. 36; 1951, [Third] California *Senate Report*, p. 9; *Novedades*, January 12, 1948.

[23] Interview with Dr. Robert J. Schroeder, Los Angeles County Livestock Department Director, and Cecil Lewis, USDA, September 11, 1961, Los Angeles, California.

[24] *El Universal*, October 9, 1947; *Novedades*, January 10, 1948.

[25] USDA, ARA, Press Release, July 23, 1947, and August 4, 1947, [First] California *Senate Report*, pp. 395, 401; *Excelsior*, September 24 and 26, 1947;

complaints continued about the slowness of indemnity payments, and some campesinos persisted in the belief that foot-and-mouth disease did not exist in Mexico. These skeptics fell prey to charlatans peddling magic elixirs, which in turn deterred eradication and contributed to the spread of the malady.

Despite CMAPEFA efforts, the spread of aftosa continued, and by June, 1947, an additional 500,000 head of livestock required destruction for effective eradication. Cattlemen began to ask that vaccination be used as a control measure, and the Ministry of Agriculture dispatched envoys to explain that slaughter still remained the most effective method. The campaign slowed in September, 1947, when the *fiestas patrias* (Mexico's Independence Day, September 16) pulled army contingents away from quarantine stations for duty in parades and in the cities. Mexican regional politicos, including the governors of affected areas, their presidentes municipales, and other local officials, met and declared their full support for CMAPEFA efforts.[26]

Mexico also faced a closed border to the south. Guatemala increased border patrol activities and charged that the United States was more interested in eradicating infection in those areas closest to its own borders than in concentrating on Veracruz and areas farther south. Guatemalan complaints to the contrary, Chiapas, Aguascalientes, Zacatecas, and San Luis Potosí were declared free of infection, and Oaxaca contained only small loci of infection. Control animals were introduced into the area to assure the efficacy of disinfection, and cattle from the clean zone were imported to restock the area.[27]

Progress in the first year of the campaign was checkered, but substantive advances were made in the eradication process. Bureaucratic sluggishness and the subjective nature of Mexican politics, according to Dr. M. R. Clarkson, accounted in part for the

USDA, ARA, Press Release, April 26, 1947, Camargo Archives; Minutes of CMAPEFA Meeting, May 6 and 7, 1947, Camargo Archives.

[26] *Excelsior*, June 25 and September 22, 1947; Minutes of CMAPEFA Meeting, July 30, 1947, Camargo Archives; B. T. Simms, "Changes in the Foot-and-Mouth Program," December 3, 1947, Camargo Archives; *El Universal*, October 9, 1947.

[27] *Excelsior*, October 11, 18, and 22, 1947.

initial slowness of the campaign. He declared: "The Central Government has what is to me a rather unfathomable arrangement with the governors of the various states. . . . In many ways, they seem to have full power, and in other ways they seem helpless, and the governors of the states can control their people independently of the principal Government." Some United States congressmen expressed indignation over Mexico's political complexities and urged that the mess be straightened out. General Charles Corlett, special adviser to the secretary of agriculture, stated, however, that the reformation could not be made abruptly: "You have got to be very patient with them. At the conferences we attended, they don't delegate authority. . . . We also know of instances of where the governor has let the Presidente down, and you are going to run into those things all the time. It is a thing requiring great patience."[28]

Mexico and the United States made a unique scientific contribution to the eradication of foot-and-mouth disease, for, as the first year of the campaign closed, total outright slaughter was abandoned. Its replacement by a combined slaughter-vaccination program necessitated amendment of the agreement between Mexico and the United States, because experimentation with live viruses had been specifically prohibited. The amendment process merely required action by the secretaries of agriculture, and plans soon began for a vaccine-producing laboratory in Mexico. Both countries continued to maintain that the most efficacious method was slaughter, and the United States adamantly contended that any other technique was as yet unproved. Yet fear of being asked by Mexico to withdraw and the latent threat implicit in such a withdrawal forced the United States to acquiesce in demands from the Mexican countryside for vaccine. Vaccination entailed giving "all susceptible animals in the affected area" temporary immunization that would starve the virus for lack of targets.[29]

[28] Simms Statement, Clarkson Statement, and Corlett Statement, *House Hearings*, pp. 3, 38, 50–51.
[29] Comisión, *Fiebre aftosa*, p. 31; Minutes of CMAPEFA Meeting, November 27, 1947, Camargo Archives; Ceremonia de la Creación del Consejo Consultivo para la Preparación de la Vacuna anti-aftosa, January 12, 1948, Camargo Archives (hereafter cited as Ceremonia); Corlett Statement, *House Hearings*, p. 58; Simms, "Changes in the Foot-and-Mouth Program," Camargo Archives; 1951, [Third] California *Senate Report*, p. 8.

Problems of production and procurement of adequate vaccine initially caused difficulties, and CMAPEFA was forced to look abroad for assistance. England sent advisers, and vaccines arrived from Holland, Switzerland, Argentina, and Denmark. Mexican scientists also visited England and South America, and experimentation began even before the slaughter operations terminated. In January, 1948, vaccine production embarked on a high-risk, unprecedented course. CMAPEFA codirector Oscar Flores told Mexican scientists that they "symbolized" the hopes of the Mexican people. "Into your hands we entrust the success of the· campaign." A Consejo Consultivo (Consultative Council) was formed under Fernando Camargo to regulate the flow of foreign vaccine into Mexico.[30]

With the creation of a technical and administrative mechanism to undertake development of a suitable vaccine and to keep Mexico from becoming a dumping ground for foreign biologicals of unknown or questionable efficacy, an expansion of facilities was needed. The handling of live virus was dangerous, and a safe location was necessary to limit new outbreaks in and around the Federal District. Two locations in addition to San Jacinto were readied to receive experimental livestock from northern aftosa-free states.[31]

By May, 1948, vaccine production in Mexico was sufficient to allow the cessation of vaccine imports from abroad. Vaccination was begun in selected areas under close inspection, but production was slow at first because of limited facilities for the testing and storage of vaccine. Space limitations notwithstanding, production increased until, by the end of October, 1948, 1 million doses were ready for use in the field; by the end of January, 1949, monthly production had doubled.[32]

[30] El Universal and Excelsior, September 25, 1947; H. F. Wilkins, "Report of the Committee on Foot-and-Mouth Disease," United States Livestock Sanitary Association, n.d. [Third] California Senate Report, p. 31; Comisión, Fiebre aftosa, p. 23; Ceremonia, Camargo Archives.

[31] Minutes of Consejo Consultivo Meeting, January 23 and 27, 1948; CMAPEFA, Boletín de Prensa, January 21, 1948; Camargo to Flores, February 8, 1948, Camargo Archives.

[32] USDA, ARA, Press Releases, May 10, October 29, 1948, and February 7, 1949, [Second] California Senate Report, pp. 30, 40, 50; C. R. Omer and C. A. Manthei to Flores and M. S. Shahan, June 1, 1948, Camargo Archives.

The great need for vaccine production forced CMAPEFA to look for still more facilities. A site was selected in Palo Alto, D.F., thirteen kilometers north of Mexico City on the México-Toluca Highway. Dignitaries from the United States, Europe, and South America were invited to the inauguration of the facility on September 1, 1949. It gave CMAPEFA a laboratory comparable to those in Pirbright, England and elsewhere in the world, facilitated improved typification and virus identification, and made distinction between aftosa and vesicular stomatitis more readily available. However, the exigencies of the campaign did not allow for the transfer of vaccine production and testing facilities from San Jacinto and San Angel to Palo Alto. Production continued at San Jacinto, and virus typification and testing were conducted at Palo Alto.[33]

Production of the vital vaccine continued at a rapid pace. By the end of 1950 commission laboratories had manufactured 53,524,000 doses of vaccine. In 1948, 1949, and 1950, 15 million head of livestock (including sheep, goats, and pigs) received 60,054,962 doses, the objective being three vaccinations a year at intervals of three to four months. Initially vaccine production and vaccination of susceptible stock met with technical problems such as testing for innocuity, potency, and amount of dosage. Once stabilized through rigid testing procedures in both the laboratory and the field, production became a mathematical process. Palo Alto was to become the headquarters of the Dirección General de Investigaciones Pecuarias, with functions expanded beyond the study of vesicular viruses. Artificial insemination, begun at Palo Alto during the last year of the anti-aftosa campaign, continues. The importation of animals in 1951 for breed improvement projects reversed livestock depletion in central Mexico through artificial insemination. Tests on feeds and animal diets are also conducted at Palo Alto, and vaccine is produced for *derriengue* (paralytic bat-borne rabies). The Comisión México-Americana para la Prevención de la Fiebre Aftosa (CMAPEFA) maintains laboratory facilities

[33] Report of George Kirksey, Special Representative, Joint Livestock Committee, June 10, 1949, [Third] California *Senate Report*, p. 47; USDA, ARA, Press Releases, July 29 and September 1, 1949, [Third] California *Senate Report*, pp. 48, 55–56; Camargo interview.

there to conduct tests for stomatitis and suspected outbreaks of foot-and-mouth disease.[34]

Aftosa failed to abate in Mexico by 1948; in the opinion of some observers, it even increased as a result of the new, experimental vaccination program. Congress, yielding to pressures from livestock interests in the United States, viewed the new program with skepticism and predicted that eradication was farther away than it had been before the cooperative venture began.[35] With the change in program, border patrols along the international boundary were increased in order to remove stray animals that wandered from Mexico into the United States Southwest. Inspection programs were also initiated at all ports of entry because commerce and air traffic from Mexico constituted a threat to the United States. Because aftosa is caused by a virus that is easily transported, increased vigilance was required in Mexico, and disinfection tanks were built along main Mexican highways.[36]

The vaccination campaign did not preclude slaughter of livestock in isolated outbreaks. The state of Tabasco, for instance, offered a "magnificent example" of the use of slaughter techniques that would be used in the future.[37] At the same time vaccine production continued and intensive efforts were made to revaccinate livestock. The Mexican campesino, however, frequently failed to comprehend that the vaccine was effective only temporarily and that it needed periodic readministration.[38]

There were no outstanding successes in 1948, but the situation was more favorable in 1949. Increased efforts in disseminating information won the support of the Sinarquistas, the conservative political party whose large rural following added to the growing list of CMAPEFA supporters.[39] Moreover, a rigorous inspection

[34] Comisión, *Fiebre aftosa*, pp. 35–36, 41, 61, 69; Camargo interview; "Nuevo plan para la eradicación de la fiebre aftosa," Camargo Archives.

[35] *Congressional Record*, 80th Congress, Second Session, April 7, 1948, pp. 4195 and A1028.

[36] USDA, ARA, Press Releases, June 15 and October 20, 1948, [Second] California *Senate Report*, pp. 70–72, 43; *Novedades*, January 4, 1948, provides the location of the disinfection tanks.

[37] *Novedades*, January 9, 1948.

[38] USDA, ARA, Press Release, July 5, 1950, [Third] California *Senate Report*, p. 83.

[39] Kirksey Report, June 10, 1948, [Third] California *Senate Report*, p. 47.

policy showed that by March, 1949, over three million head of stock, approximately one-third of the total in the affected area, had been inspected. Increased surveillance of transport facilities also contributed to the control of the malady.[40]

In May, 1949, aftosa struck 384 miles south of Brownsville, Texas, and CMAPEFA feared that it might sweep north and endanger the United States even more. Although the outbreak was rapidly eradicated, BAI officials emphasized the "insidious nature of foot-and-mouth disease. In spite of experiencing 29 days without evidence of active infection, this turn of events indicates the severity of the disease and the possibility of its sudden reappearance. Need for continual vigilance and precautions is apparent . . . if the plans for control and final eradication are to be successful."[41]

An outbreak in October, 1949, threatened to change the whole complexion of the campaign against foot-and-mouth disease, for a new viral type, Type O, appeared. Rapid eradication and disinfection curtailed further outbreaks, and it was announced that slaughter would again be used if Type O should reappear. The effectiveness with which CMAPEFA met the new challenge "convinced many of the program's severest critics that the efficiency and thoroughness of the organization was equal to any task which might arise." The new virus was declared eradicated in February, 1950.[42]

The prognosis for 1950 was more cheerful; vaccination efforts seemed to have been successful when no outbreaks were reported by February. The following month, a cutback in vaccination was announced, and CMAPEFA declared that it would put even greater emphasis on inspection. Initial successes brought concomitant dangers of overconfidence and complacency among the Mexican people. Mexican livestock raisers, however, feared that the vaccine cutback endangered their interests; the Asociación Nacional de Productores de Leche Pura (National Association of Milk Producers) for example, claimed that the new Palo Alto laboratory was not fulfilling its function. The dairymen claimed that a reappear-

[40] USDA, ARA, Press Releases, May 12 and 16, 1949, [Third] California Senate Report, pp. 38–39.
[41] Ibid., May 16, 1949, p. 39.
[42] Ibid., October 25, November 2, December 12, 1949, and March 29, 1950, pp. 59, 61, 69, and 74.

ance of aftosa meant that slaughter, not vaccine, would be used as the combative method.

But setbacks and technical difficulties were finally overcome: the last known infection was eliminated in August, 1951, and on September 1, 1952, Mexico was declared free of aftosa. Accordingly, the United States reopened its borders to Mexican livestock. At this time, CMAPEFA dropped the word "eradication" from its name and became the Comisión México-Americana para la Prevención de la Fiebre Aftosa, or CMAPPFA.[43]

Conquest of the virus proved temporary, however; CMAPPFA announced an outbreak in Gutiérrez Zamora, Veracruz, in May, 1953. The United States border was again closed, and the already established facilities in Mexico resumed operation. The same stringent sanitary measures were applied; in addition, a military cordon isolated the area.[44] The new control procedures proved effective. By March, 1954, the last known pocket of infection was declared eradicated, and control animals were introduced into the area. Two months later, Mexico was again declared free of aftosa.[45]

The diligent efforts of the joint commission had borne fruit. Their ultimate success, however, had been marred by persistent superstition, ignorance, greed, and gullibility. Even though the vast majority of the Mexican people supported the efforts of CMAPEFA, opposition from an intransigent minority had begun even before the United States officially gave help to Mexico. The slaughter campaign had a profound effect on the sentimental Mexican peasant who considered his few head of stock as part of his family.[46] The principal areas of opposition were Guerrero, Michoacán, and the state of México; in June, 1947, CMAPEFA temporarily pulled its forces out of Guerrero because of relentless opposition; within

[43] Kirksey Reports, March 9 and July 10, 1950, [Third] California *Senate Report*, pp. 76–77; Information Division, CMAPEFA, Press Release, March 9, 1950, ibid., p. 36; *Excelsior*, February 3, 1950, Asociación Nacional de Productores de Leche Pura to Oscar Flores, November 4, 1950, Camargo Archives.

[44] R. J. Anderson, Director, Division of Animal Disease Eradication, USDA, to author, July 11, 1961; Interview with Dr. Luis de la Torre Zarza, Comisión México-Americana para la Prevención de la Fiebre Aftosa, June 23, 1963, Palo Alto, D.F.

[45] De la Torre interview; *Excelsior*, May 24 and 25, 1953.

[46] De la Torre interview.

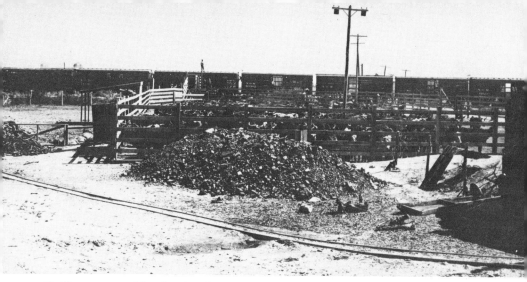

Holding pens, public slaughterhouse, Ciudad Juárez, circa 1915. Courtesy USDA, Agricultural History Branch.

Quartering carcasses, public slaughterhouse, Ciudad Juárez, circa 1915. Courtesy USDA, Agricultural History Branch.

Hereford crossbred steer, Chihuahua, Mexico, circa 1915. Courtesy USDA, Agricultural History Branch.

Cattle hacienda headquarters, Chihuahua, Mexico, circa 1915. Courtesy USDA, Agricultural History Branch.

EL "AGUA FIESTAS".

The note on the death's head Zebu jumping the fence reads, "Zebu wishes you a Happy New Year!" *El Universal*, January 1, 1947.

SILUETAS DE AUDIFFRED

El Escándalo del Día.

Out of the aftosa-infected piggy bank leaps a figure with "fraud" written on the leg. The caption states that this is the "scandal of the day." *El Universal,* October 9, 1947.

Range on the Phillips Ranch, Coahuila. Courtesy Carter Montgomery, Dallas, Texas.

Crossbred cattle, Phillips Ranch, Coahuila. Courtesy Carter Montgomery, Dallas, Texas.

Working cattle, Phillips Ranch, Coahuila. Courtesy Carter Montgomery, Dallas, Texas.

Aerial view of cattle and corrals to be used for screwworm inspection. Courtesy USDA, Agricultural History Branch.

Sorting cattle for screwworm inspection, northeastern Mexico. Note the preponderance of Zebu livestock. Courtesy USDA, Agricultural History Branch.

Plane used for spraying sterile flies over northeastern Mexico. Courtesy, USDA, Agricultural History Branch.

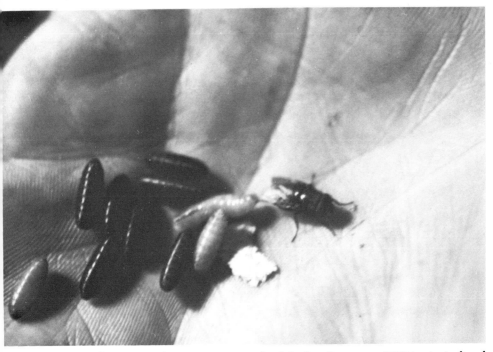

Screwworm larvae, pupae, and adult fly. Courtesy, USDA, Agricultural History Branch.

less than six months the same thing occurred in Michoacán.[47] Less sophisticated cattle raisers failed to understand the necessity of slaughter as a means of eradicating foot-and-mouth disease. Even the governor of Tlaxcala played to local discontent; for example, he stated that with Tlaxcala's 20,000 head of cattle, only 10 percent were slaughtered, and implied that slaughter was unessential to eradication.[48] Gossip and half-truths stimulated the opposition; cattle buyers often told peasants that CMAPEFA brigades paid nothing for the stock. Peasants were also informed that joint commission personnel would castrate all the old men of a village if they did not cooperate. With the initiation of vaccination, Yankeephobes in Mexico declared that eating meat from vaccinated stock rendered people sterile. This nefarious "fact" was said to constitute part of a "sinister plot of the United States to depopulate Mexico."[49]

Even religion played a part in the opposition to the anti-aftosa efforts. Rural Mexican religion, a combination of Old World faith and New World paganism, attributes much importance to holy days, saints' days, and other religious festivals. This form of veneration led to an unusual situation in Guerrero. Peasants refused to corral their stock for vaccination and inspection, stating that the animals were corraled but once a year, on October 18, San Lucas' Day. Therefore, with the support of the Mexican Army, the brigades were forced to capture, inspect, and vaccinate the cattle at different water holes.[50]

The presence and occasional ineptitude of the military engendered fear and antagonism that hindered the progress of the campaign. One soldier stationed with a quarantine and inspection unit near Guadalajara reported that the people blamed the government for the supposedly low payments they received for slaughtered

[47] Simms Statement and Corlett Statement, *House Hearings*, pp. 5–6, 53; Schroeder-Lewis interview.

[48] Comisión, *Fiebre aftosa*, pp. 29–30; Porter, *Doctor*, pp. 16–18; USDA, ARA, Press Release, May 12, 1949, [Third] California *Senate Report*, pp. 29, 51.

[49] *Excelsior*, October 23, 1947; Schroeder-Lewis interview; Kirksey Report, July 11, 1949, [Third] California *Senate Report*, p. 51.

[50] For a thorough discussion of religion in rural Mexico see Nathan L. Whetten, *Rural Mexico*; Kirksey Report, March 9, 1950, [Third] California *Senate Report*, p. 77.

stock and on one occasion attempted to ambush him and other soldiers who had done the actual shooting.[51]

Opposition to the campaign had its violent manifestations, often led by petty demagogues who opposed United States participation in the joint effort. In June, 1947, one Mexican veterinarian was killed by peasants who opposed the slaughter of livestock.[52] Three months later another Mexican veterinarian and six soldiers met their deaths at Senguio, Michoacán; drunken peasants hacked up the seven men with machetes. The massacre led to temporary suspension of field operations, the strengthening of military forces in Michoacán, and an increased education program. Some residents of Senguio opposed the participation of the United States, even though cattle in and around Senguio had not been slaughtered. The incident also had political repercussions: the ruling Partido Revolucionario Institucional (PRI) blamed the opposition Sinarquistas for the murder. The latter in return accused the PRI of attempting to discredit a party that threatened the hegemony of the PRI in Mexico.[53] Speedy action caused comment in Mexico, for many crimes remained outstanding while, according to *Excelsior*, rapid execution of justice came to the Indians of Senguio. One hundred persons eventually were arrested for the massacre and received prison sentences.[54]

One of the most gruesome examples of the gullibility of the campesinos occurred on January 31, 1949, when Robert Proctor, a twenty-two-year-old livestock inspector from Tucson, Arizona, was killed at Temascalcingo in the state of México. Hundreds of drunken peasants rushed Proctor's brigade; all but Proctor escaped. He was handed over to drunken Indian women who proceeded to kill him with knives. Mexican officials quickly investigated and made arrests. The prosecution asked for capital punishment, and *Excelsior* reported that death sentences were given to twenty-eight persons. United States officials in both Mexico and the United States com-

[51] De la Torre interview; Oscar Lewis, *The Children of Sanchez*, p. 197.

[52] *Excelsior*, June 17. 1947.

[53] *Excelsior*, September 4, 19, 20, 22, and 27, and October 3, 9, and 31, 1947; *La Prensa* (Mexico City), October 8, 1947.

[54] *El Universal*, October 9, 1947; USDA, ARA, Press Release, September 20, 1947, [First] California *Senate Report*, p. 412; De la Torre interview.

mented favorably on the cooperation and efficiency of the Mexican authorities.[55]

Opposition to United States participation began early, and was occasionally violent. Many organized cattlemen's groups complained bitterly. One delegation from Michoacán told President Alemán that he should be cognizant of the "true feelings of the public which says that the campaign that extinguishes agricultural wealth is dictated by the United States government," which could not afford to have aftosa on its soil and "does not vacillate in condemning the nation [Mexico] to misery." Moreover, they added, the Good Neighbor Policy was dead because a good neighbor does not destroy another's economy.[56]

Some Mexico City journals began to print anti-Yankee complaints. One poem in *Excelsior*, for example, excoriated the United States for acting in its own interests:

"Más Vale Tarde . . . "

Cualquier res aftosa cura [el rifle sanitario]
y ya no se vuelva a enfermarse
de dicho mal se asegura
quien no puede equivocarse.

Y ahora en México se ve
como una triste verdad
¡qué ha sido peor el remedio
que la enfermedad!

Se mata sin compasión
nuestro ganado bovino
sólo para la protección
del ganado del vecino.

Si la aftosa cunde allá
el vecino ganadero
de seguro perderá
mientras la ataca, dinero.

<hr />

[55] USDA, ARA, Press Release, February 7, 1949, [Second] California *Senate Report*, pp. 48–49; *Excelsior*, February 7, 1950.
[56] *Excelsior*, June 10, 1947.

Y si allá no cunde, entiende
que esa gente, bien pagada
se hará más rica vendiendo
cueros, y leche enlatada.

Asi, si el vecino ayuda
solo lo hace por su bien
y surge al pueblo una duda
¿quién esta ayudando a quien?

Por eso, si éxito alcanza
aquella vacuna exótica
el suspender la matanza
será un labor patriótica.

Y aunque algo tarde empieza
¡aún será cosa oportuna
defender nuestra riqueza vacuna
con vacuna![57]

"Better Late than Never—"

Whichever aftosa infected animal is cured
[by the sanitary rifle]
will never again sicken
from that malady, rest assured,
there will be no mistake.

And now in Mexico can be seen
the sad truth
that the cure was worse than the sickness.

Our cattle are killed
without compassion
solely for the protection
of the neighbor's livestock.

Should aftosa spread there,
the neighboring cattleman
would surely lose money
while he attacked it.

[57] Simms Statement, *House Hearings*, pp. 6–7; *Excelsior*, September 4, 1947.

And if it doesn't spread there,
those well-paid people
will get even richer
selling hides and canned milk.

Thus, if the neighbor helps,
it's only for his benefit.
And the people ask,
who is helping whom?

For that reason, if that
exotic vaccine is successful
the suspension of slaughter
would be a patriotic act.

And even though it begins somewhat late,
wouldn't this be an opportune thing
to defend our livestock riches
with vaccine!

Even temporary cessation of slaughter failed to stifle opposition, for if a vaccinated animal died, demagogues blamed the United States vaccine, even though only Mexican veterinarians and technicians had administered it. Moreover, the deep-seated animosity toward the United States led many people to prefer aftosa to United States activity in Mexico. Many acts of violence were performed in an attempt to embarrass the United States.[58]

Mexico's political milieu perplexed the United States contingent of CMAPEFA; the power of caciques and *caciquismo* (bossism) was blatant and unfamiliar.[59] If convinced that the anti-aftosa campaign would benefit them, the local caciques cooperated; if not, they led their followers into opposition. It became necessary, therefore, to expedite municipal progress through the caciques. Also, the tenuous alliances between state governors and local officials restricted the amount of pressure for cooperation the governors could bring to bear on the caciques.[60]

[58] Conference on Vaccine Production, Minutes, January 3, 1948, Camargo Archives; Clarkson Statement, *House Hearings*, p. 29; Kirksey Report, August 10, 1949, [Third] California *Senate Report*, pp. 54–55.

[59] Auró Saldaña, *Factores*, pp. 27–28.

[60] Corlett Statement and Statement of Albert K. Mitchell, *House Hearings*, pp. 49, 66–67.

Although the Mexican political system is essentially dominated by one party, the PRI, opposition parties are tolerated so long as they do not threaten PRI hegemony. One of these parties, the Partido de Acción Nacional (National Action Party), or PAN, planned a visit to Mexico City from La Piedad, Michoacán, to complain about electoral irregularities. The trip was cancelled by PRI officials, allegedly because of the danger of spreading aftosa. Another PAN group in Michoacán found that a meeting was cancelled, again for fear of spreading aftosa. Members of PAN, reported *Excelsior*, refrained from gathering for fear that "perhaps the 'sanitary rifle' would be used on them."[61]

In an attempt to quell opposition, Secretary of Agriculture Ortiz Garza announced in January, 1947, that aftosa would soon be defeated.[62] The army, however, appraised the situation more realistically and ordered all military personnel to act as media agents for distributing information on aftosa, including the means used to eradicate it.[63] After the Senguio massacre, CMAPEFA appointed *informadores*, or information men, for this task. These men, many of whom spoke the Indian languages and dialects, were dispatched into hostile areas to explain in detail the methods and rationale of eradicating and controlling foot-and-mouth disease. In cases where information men could not speak the Indian dialects, trouble usually ensued, including violence.[64]

Early in the campaign, President Alemán himself appealed to the citizenry for help. On a trip to the Bajío region, he underwent disinfection procedures as an example to a reluctant peasantry. Despite an intransigent minority of caciques, local political groups usually cooperated, and commission brigades used them to gain campesino support. Cattlemen's groups were also helpful in the recruitment of field personnel for local operations.[65]

[61] *Excelsior*, June 18, 1947.

[62] *El Universal*, January 8, 1947.

[63] Comandancia Militar, Reglamento, March 16, 1947, Palo Alto Library.

[64] USDA, ARA, Press Release, May 12, 1949, [Third] California *Senate Report*, p. 39; Schroeder-Lewis interview.

[65] *Excelsior*, June 10, 1947; Interview with Dr. Fred Major, Inspector in Charge of Animal Disease Eradication, USDA, El Paso, Texas, July 16, 1962; Interview with Dr. Donald M. Williams, Codirector, CMAPPFA, July 2, 1962, Mexico City.

With increased publicity efforts, especially after the Senguio incident, opposition was appreciably reduced by mid-1949. A film was made for propaganda purposes and by October, 1947, was being shown in theaters around Toluca.[66] The cooperation of field personnel in dispelling fear also helped break down latent opposition, and radio and newspapers were somewhat useful in reaching the people. But because some newspapers became alarmist, official brochures were used increasingly. One such brochure explained in detail the advantage of vaccination:

Campesino:

Lee con atención este folleto para que conozca la verdad de como se hace y se prueba la vacuna que salvará a tus animales de la terrible fiebre aftosa.

La vacuna es preparada con el mayor cuidado por médicos y hombres de ciencia que luchan para acabar con la fiebre aftosa. *Es mentira* que la vacuna haga mal a los animales. *No creas* quienes tratan de engañarte y ayuda a las brigadas de vacunación dando facilidades para que tus animales sean vacunados.

Es por México, tu patria, que tienes la obligación de vacunar a tus animales y ayudar a los vacunadores.

Solo con la vacuna se ayudará a salvar a tu ganado. La vacuna y que tus animales sean vacunados no te costara ni un centavo. . . .

. . . te aseguramos que la vacuna contra la fiebre aftosa *no enflaquece al ganado, no lo inutiliza para que pueda reproducirse, no ocasiona los abortos, no es dañina para tus animales y sobre todo no te cuesta ni un solo centavo.*[67]

Campesino:

Read attentively the folder so that you will know the truth of how the vaccine is made and tested that will save your livestock from terrible foot-and-mouth disease.

The vaccine is prepared with absolute care by doctors and men of science who struggle to do away with foot-and-mouth disease. *It is a lie*

[66] Comisión, *Fiebre aftosa*, p. 20; *Excelsior*, May 29, June 18, and October 8, 1947; Direccion General de Investigaciones Pecuarias, Press Release no. 211 [n.d.], Camargo Archives; Schroeder-Lewis interview; Major interview; Auró Saldaña, *Factores*, p. 26. According to Camargo, news reporters produced such distortions that the peasants became alarmed; thus the government was forced to manage the news by 1948. Camargo interview; Simms Statement, *House Hearings*, p. 5; USDA, ARA, Press Release, October 20, 1948, [Second] California *Senate Report*, pp. 41–42; *Novedades*, January 24, 1948.

[67] CMAPEFA, *¿QUE SABE [USTED] DE LA VACUNA CONTRA LA AFTOSA?* Palo Alto Library, Palo Alto, D.F.

that the vaccine will hurt your animals. *Do not believe* those who attempt to deceive you and help the vaccine brigades by providing facilities for the vaccination of your animals.

It is for Mexico, your fatherland, that you have the obligation to vaccinate your animals and to help the vaccinators. *Only with the vaccine* can your animals be saved. The vaccine and the vaccination of your animals will not cost you a single cent.

We assure you that the anti-aftosa vaccine *will not cause your cattle to lose weight, will not make them sterile, will not abort them, is not dangerous for your animals, and above all does not cost a single cent.*

Mexican schools and the clergy joined CMAPEFA in gaining popular cooperation. Schools taught their students how to recognize foot-and-mouth disease and the procedures being used for combating the malady. In addition, the secretary of public education dispatched "cultural brigades" to isolated areas to carry information to the campesinos. In April, 1947, the archbishop of Mexico ordered his clergy to cooperate and tell the faithful of the "sacrifice necessary to limit the diffusion of the pestilence to other regions [of the Republic] and . . . to exterminate it radically." Ecclesiastics in Querétaro distributed a pastoral letter that asked for full cooperation.[68] Priests harangued from the pulpits, often referring to foot-and-mouth disease as the *castigo de Dios* (God's punishment) visited upon a sinful nation by a righteous and angry God; only cooperation could lift the penance from the shoulders of Mexico.[69]

Codirector Maurice Shahan praised Mexican administrative honesty generally in August, 1947.[70] Nevertheless, although mass media, field personnel, government agencies, and interested private groups had helped reduce opposition by 1950, an undercurrent of avarice and corruption had slowed the campaign. The *mordida* (bribe) was used regularly by cattlemen to ship their cattle out of the infected zone or to prevent the slaughter of livestock. Corrupt military officials and a few civilian appraisers of livestock, though a minority, lined their pockets with CMAPEFA funds by giving low evaluations, which contributed to the reluctance of the peasants to bring in their animals. *Excelsior* commented that brigades

[68] *El Universal*, April 4, 1947, and October 9, 1947; *Novedades*, April 2, 1947; *Excelsior*, October 3, 1947.

[69] Camargo interview.

[70] *Ultimas Noticias*, August 28, 1947.

in Jalisco were "committing real sacks" of local pocketbooks.[71] An outstanding example was General Félix Ireta Viveros, senator from Michoacán, who became involved in a scandal known as the *danza de los cerdos* (dance of the pigs). Thousands of slaughtered pigs supposedly had been buried in trenches in Zinepécuaro and Morelia; when the trenches were uncovered, however, only a few hundred pigs were found. Oscar Flores initiated legal proceedings against Ireta, who was accused of participating in a scheme to claim compensation for pigs that had not been slaughtered. The attorney general dispatched a "special agent . . . to confront the situation and the powerful men who would pretend to blotch Mexico's prestige. . . ." With formal charges pending, Ireta asked the Senate to excuse him for two months in order to prepare a defense. Former President Lázaro Cárdenas, also of Michoacán, quoted in the leftist Mexico City tabloid *La Prensa*, asked for vigorous punishment for all guilty parties without "distinctions as to class or position"; Ireta retorted that PRI officials merely wanted to use him as a scapegoat to smear him politically. The Mexican Senate, however, asked for maximum penalties for the guilty parties.[72] Ireta and his accomplices were soon known to government investigators, and an official indictment charged them with attempting to defraud the government of 244,320 pesos. Ireta was then arraigned and condemned by the grand jury of the Chamber of Deputies, which declared that "this is the opportunity to prove that Mexico's public life is morally directed." A warrant was issued for Ireta's arrest, he was ousted from the Senate, and he voluntarily presented himself at the Public Ministry in Morelia. Although he faced incontrovertible evidence, he continued to protest his innocence until October 24, 1947, when he confessed to the falsification of documents. The PRI praised Ireta's expulsion from the Senate, and *La Prensa* pointed to Ireta as "a typical example of the political medium [of Mexico]" based on audacity, frauds, and *compadrazgo*.[73]

[71] Kirksey Reports of July 11, 1949, and January 10, 1950, [Third] California *Senate Report*, pp. 51, 71; Auró Saldaña, *Factores*, pp. 28–29; *Excelsior*, May 12, July 29, and August 10, 1947.

[72] *El Universal*, October 9, 1947; *Excelsior*, October 7 and 9, 1947; *La Prensa*, October 9, 1947.

[73] *Excelsior*, October 9, 16, 18, 21, 22, 23, 24, and 25, 1947; *La Prensa*, October 9, 1947; see also Whetten, *Rural Mexico*.

Thus serious opposition was gradually overcome, and in the process many aides from the United States became aware of deep differences between their own culture and that south of the Rio Grande. Mexican politics, based on caudillismo, caciquismo, and subjective personal relationships, often perplexed and outraged United States officials. Field workers, however, made adjustments and learned to work within the culture of Mexico.

By 1950, direct costs to the United States alone had reached $120 million for the eradication of foot-and-mouth disease. The money not only eradicated disease but also enabled researchers to develop knowledge about the nature of the malady and contributed significantly to development of a potential method—the vaccination plus limited slaughter employed in the revised campaign—for control and eradication.[74] Presented with a necessity, the United States sagaciously entered into a cooperative effort that protected both its own interests and those of Mexico.

The outbreak of aftosa in Mexico in late 1946 underscored the mutual dependency between the two countries. The United States provided a market for feeder cattle from northern Mexico while Mexico supplied the needed additional cattle for feedlots in the United States. It became apparent that one could not subsist without the other. Opposition to the anti-aftosa campaign came not from northern Mexico but from areas in the central and southern zones unaffected by market considerations.

Although statistical data are unavailable, it is clear that the number of opponents of the CMAPEFA campaign was small in comparison with the number who acquiesced in the necessary slaughter of infected and directly exposed, susceptible stock. Subsequent rumors about vaccination emerged as last-ditch efforts to sabotage eradication measures. Patience and a carefully directed education campaign eventually convinced the majority of campesinos that neither they nor their livestock would suffer inordinately if the vaccine was administered.

The campaign against foot-and-mouth disease contributed to Mexican modernization, for mules and tractors began to replace

[74] Wilkins Report, [Third] California *Senate Report*, pp. 31–32; Schroeder-Lewis interview.

oxen in central Mexico. The malady disposed of some inferior stock, which were replaced by better stock, and quality was also improved by the artificial insemination station at Palo Alto. Successful Mexican–United States cooperation also underscored how far each country had come in its relations with its neighbor, for initial suspicion had eventually yielded to cautious trust.

Finally, the cooperative effort marked the first and only total commitment by two hemispheric neighbors to eradicate a threat to their economies and standards of living. Political differences notwithstanding, both countries actively undertook to help each other at a time of crisis, and their cooperation served as a model for the entire hemisphere.

5. Adversity and Recovery, 1946–1960

THE administration of Miguel Alemán (1946–1952) aimed at greater efficiency in all facets of the national economy. Greater emphasis upon efficiency of production led Alemán and his political coterie to shift the emphasis from the small ejidos to the maximum use of resources. In this context, the demands of the marketplace played a significant role.

The ending of World War II in 1945 and the immediate onslaught of foot-and-mouth disease in 1946 forced Mexico to reevaluate the condition of her cattle industry. Disastrous as aftosa was for Mexico, the long campaign to eradicate the disease nevertheless forced Mexico into herd improvement. As a result, Mexican cattle became increasingly important in trade with the United States and to some degree also with the rest of Latin America. Countries in Central America called upon Mexican expertise and Mexican stock to build up their own livestock industries. Northern Mexico through the postwar period continued to produce for an export market based almost exclusively in the United States.

Under Alemán, the definition of grazing lands became increasingly confused, for while he moved toward a productive, market-oriented rather than subsistence type of agriculture, the technocrats within his administration were not inclined to discard altogether the concept of small farms and collective ejidos.

By using the 1938 decrees of unaffectability and revising the definitions of grazing land, Alemán permitted increases in the size of landholdings used for pasturage. Thus, lands that could support up to 500 head of cattle were permitted to vary in size from 5,000 to 8,000 hectares. These allowances took into consideration the arid and semiarid conditions in northern Mexico, for this much land was necessary for the essentially pastoral nature of the region's cattle industry. The shift from rural to urban labor and from agricultural to industrial productivity gave increasing support to the concept of the *pequeño propietario* (small landholder) as opposed to the less functional ejido. To achieve greater agricultural production, irrigation projects moved water to formerly arid lands, thus helping small farmers, some of whom were part of the Alemán political mechanism.[1]

Mexico's battle against foot-and-mouth disease had devastated her cattle industry. Throughout the country, the quarantine and slaughter of infected cattle and the prohibition on exports to international markets left that segment of the agricultural economy with a sense of devastation and an actual loss. The establishment of canneries in northern Mexico somewhat alleviated the plight of the industry. Acting as an intermediary, the USDA bought Mexico's canned beef and sold it in turn to the United Kingdom. In all, the British purchased over 6 million pounds of this canned beef. Other markets absorbed the remaining 214 million pounds of beef at four cents per pound.[2]

Mexico looked forward to the termination of the anti-aftosa campaign. In August, 1952, one month before the quarantine was lifted, Mexico prepared to export 300,000 head of livestock to the United States. Though understandably enthusiastic about the prospect of a reopened northern market, Mexican cattlemen were nevertheless dependent upon range conditions in the United States: if periodic drought continued to plague the southwest, Mexican cattle could not be accommodated.[3] Not until 1960 would Mexico again use the United States as a major outlet for its export cattle.

Aftosa hindered but did not stop the development of the Mexican cattle industry. While the disease took its toll of livestock in Mexico, it created an opportunity for the slaughter of inferior stock. Mexico began to build higher-quality breeding herds in order

[1] Frank Brandenburg, *The Making of Modern Mexico*, pp. 105–107; United Nations Comisión Económica para América Latina, *La industria de la carne de ganado bovino en México*, p. 18.

[2] Florence C. Lister and Robert H. Lister, *Chihuahua: Storehouse of Storms*, p. 285; USDA Press Release, June 13, 1951, Agricultural History Branch Files, U.S. Department of Agriculture, Washington, D.C.

[3] USDA Press Release, August 5, 1952, Agricultural History Branch Files.

to restock the country once the disease waned. Between 1946 and 1952, Mexico imported large numbers of breeding cattle. (See Table 5 in the appendix.) Including the infamous 327 Zebu bulls from Brazil, Mexico imported for breeding purposes a total of 3,305 head of livestock in 1946; the remainder that year, nearly 3,000 head, came from the United States. The cattle carried a total value of 2,648,334 pesos (the peso then being valued at four to the dollar).[4] In 1949–1950 Mexico imported 1,003 cattle, again mainly from the United States, for use as breeding animals.[5] In 1951 Mexico decreased her imports slightly. She brought in only 641 head of livestock, 90 percent of them from the United States.[6] The following year, with aftosa definitely on the decline, Mexico almost tripled imports from the United States, increased purchases from Canada, and added Cuba to the list of suppliers.[7]

The minor resurgence of aftosa in Mexico in 1953 did not immediately slow the program of livestock improvement; in that year Mexico imported almost four thousand head of cattle for breeding purposes. In 1954, however, her imports were reduced by half, probably a reflection of the recurrence of aftosa in September, 1953.[8]

Between 1955 and 1960, Mexico radically accelerated imports in order to replenish the cattle regions of both central and northern Mexico. Beginning in 1956, Mexico brought in more than ten thousand head of livestock valued at over 23 million pesos.[9] In 1959 she began to diversify her imports: Mexican purchases of foreign cattle amounted to almost eleven thousand head, equally divided between dairy and breeding stock.[10] In many instances dairy stock also provided a basis for the production of beef calves through the crossing of beef-type bulls with predominantly Holstein cows. (Full statistics are available in Table 5 in the appendix.)

Suppliers of breeding stock to Mexico during the years 1946–1960 were in an enviable position. For five years of that period,

[4] *Anuario estadístico de comercio exterior*, 1945–1946, p. 34.
[5] Ibid., 1949–1950, p. 60.
[6] Ibid., 1952, p. 12.
[7] Ibid., 1952, p. 12.
[8] Ibid., 1954, p. 14.
[9] Ibid., 1956, p. 14.
[10] Ibid., 1960, p. 14.

they did not have to buy Mexican cattle in return for selling breeding stock to Mexican cattlemen. In 1946, the last good year for Mexican exports to the United States, almost 500,000 head of Mexican cattle, primarily feeder stock, were sold to be finished in the United States and sold as slaughter cattle. Again, the principal source of beef was northern Mexico.[11]

Relaxation of quarantine restrictions as a result of the first eradication of aftosa in 1952 brought about a reopening of the border. Between September and December, 1952, Mexico sold 122,000 head of livestock to the United States. In the first nine months of 1953, Mexico exported approximately 135,000 head to the United States. The resurgence of aftosa between September, 1953, and December, 1954, gave Mexico little opportunity to regain her foreign market.[12] Yet the demand for Mexican beef persisted in the United States: in 1955 Mexican exports climbed to over 243,000.[13] By 1958 pressures in the United States placed increasing demands on Mexican producers of feeder cattle. In that year 313,000 head of Mexican cattle crossed the border into the United States.[14]

Export-import statistics fail to convey, however, the total number of cattle consumed in Mexico both for internal use and for sale to foreign markets. On a national scale, beginning in 1949 at the high point of the campaign against foot-and-mouth disease, 870,-000 head of cattle weighing approximately 131 million kilograms and valued at nearly 276 million pesos. In 1953 this figure climbed steadily, reaching over 1.3 million head valued at approximately 648 million pesos and weighing almost 197 million kilograms.[15]

For the next seven years (1954–1960), domestic consumption of Mexican beef reflected a marked increase of beef in the diet of a burgeoning population. In 1955 Mexico slaughtered over 1.3 million head of cattle valued at nearly 890 million pesos (reflecting a devaluation in 1954) and weighing over 206 million kilograms. Cattle slaughtered in Mexico for domestic consumption between

[11] Ibid., 1945–1946, p. 12.

[12] Ibid., 1952, p. 12; 1954, p. 356.

[13] Ibid., 1956, p. 392.

[14] Ibid., 1958, p. 509.

[15] Unnumbered typescript materials, General Files, Dirección General de Estadística, Mexico City.

1955 and 1960 increased approximately 30 percent. In 1960 Mexican slaughterhouses processed over 1.8 million head of stock weighing almost 274 million kilograms and valued at nearly 2 billion pesos.[16] (See Table 9 in the appendix.)

The same increase occurred at the provincial level. In Chihuahua, for example, the largest producer of beef cattle in the Republic, slaughterhouses in 1949 processed over 46,000 head of cattle valued at over 12 million pesos and weighing almost 6.3 kilograms. In 1960 Chihuahuan consumption jumped to 81,000 head valued at over 90 million pesos and weighing over 13 million kilograms.[17] The state of Coahuila, another major producer in the northern tier of Mexican states, reflected the same growth. In 1949 Coahuilan abbatoirs slaughtered over 32,000 head of cattle weighing over 4.4 million kilograms and valued at 8.5 million pesos. By 1960 Coahuila had undergone wide fluctuations in the slaughter of cattle. From a high point of over 45,000 head in 1953 she slumped to 35,000 in 1955, climbed to almost 48,000 head in 1957, and leveled off at 38,402 head in 1960. This last yield weighed over 5.3 million kilograms and was valued at over 32 million pesos.[18]

The Federal District, or Mexico City and its immediate environs, grew steadily as industrialization attracted increasing numbers of people from the countryside. This growth placed pressure on cattlemen in Mexico to supply more beef for the urban population. Beginning in 1949, slaughterhouses in Mexico City killed 211,000 head of cattle weighing almost 33 million kilograms and valued at over 65 million pesos. This figure was almost 25 percent of the total slaughtered throughout the entire country. In 1958 the figure almost tripled, reaching over 534,000 head, or approximately 30 percent of the national total. (See Table 9 in the appendix.) In 1960 the number of cattle for the Federal District slumped to nearly 500,000 head weighing almost 76 million kilograms and valued at approximately 471 million pesos.[19]

Generally, the demands of the Federal District took increasing precedence over the rest of the country. The number of cattle

16 Ibid.
17 Ibid.
18 Ibid.
19 Ibid.

slaughtered in the Federal District was disproportionate for the population of the district did not grow at the same rate as the number of cattle slaughtered. In short, the Mexican government pursued the same assumption it had in the past: that those benefits accruing to Mexico City undoubtedly benefited the nation generally; provincial areas would be called upon to make sacrifices for the advantage of Mexico City.

Cattle increased in value between 1946 and 1960. Much of this increase, however, was illusory, for Mexico devalued the peso in 1954. Thus, cattle valued at 6.2 billion pesos in 1950 jumped in value by 1960 to over 21 billion pesos, showing an increase of almost 15 billion pesos.[20]

As cattle numbers and values increased throughout the period 1946–1960, so too did land available for pasturage. In 1930 Mexico's pasturelands of more than 5 hectares per unit amounted to nearly 63 million hectares. Ejido lands used for pasturage reached 3.6 million hectares. In 1940 the number of large units of land (over 5 hectares) had been reduced radically; pasturelands of more than five hectares per unit amounted to over 45 million hectares while small units topped 83,000. The most remarkable increase in national pasturelands between 1930 and 1940 came in ejido holdings. Mexican ejidos, as a result of Cárdenas' reforms, now possessed over 10 million hectares of pastures. The same pattern prevailed from 1940 to 1950. After an initial slump between 1930 and 1940, large units of pastureland rose to over 50 million hectares by 1950. Small units remained relatively stable, though ejidos experienced another significant increase, reaching nearly 17 million hectares of national pastureland distributed among them.[21] (See Table 11 in the appendix.)

Northern Mexico—which the *III Censo Agrícola y Ganadero* (Third Agricultural and Cattle Census) defined as Chihuahua, Coahuila, Durango, Nuevo León, Zacatecas, San Luis Potosí, and Tamaulipas—possessed fully two-thirds of the national pasturelands in the censuses of 1930, 1940, and 1950. From one-half to two-thirds of the ejido lands were located in those states. On the

[20] *IV Censo agrícola y ganadero,* 1965, p. xviii.
[21] *III Censo agrícola y ganadero,* 1950, p. 9.

other hand, only about 15 percent of the small-unit pastures could be found in the northern tier of states.[22] This distribution in part reflected the unsuitability of the ejido system for the commercial production of export cattle in northern Mexico. (For full details, see Table 12 in the appendix.) Chihuahua alone possessed over 13 million hectares of pasturelands in units of five hectares or more in 1930; this number dropped by over 1 million hectares in 1940 but rose to 14 million by 1950. The ejido lands multiplied partly as a result of political commitments to agrarian reform.[23]

Within another decade (by 1960), national pasturelands in Mexico increased to over 59 million hectares in units larger than five hectares. Small units also jumped markedly after 1950. In fact, from nearly 83,000 hectares of pastureland in 1950, small units had increased by 1960 to over 350,000 hectares. In the same decade, ejido pastures jumped another 3 million hectares. In 1950 Mexico possessed over 67 million hectares of pastureland; by 1960 she had increased this by nearly 20 percent, almost 12 million hectares.[24] Pasturelands in Chihuahua and the north in general remained reasonably stable.[25]

Bare statistics, however, fail to convey the actual force behind the increase in ejido lands and the loss of lands by the large landholders. As early as the Revolution, various haciendas had come under fire from revolutionary regimes. One of these, the Palomas Land and Cattle Company, continued to receive attention. In June, 1947, President Alemán ordered the secretary of agriculture and husbandry to occupy Palomas lands and divide them among various colonists. On May 2, 1951, funds obtained through the sale of Palomas lands were reinvested in the north for the establishment of agricultural colonies. Rumors of corruption in the disposition of these lands abounded throughout the period. President Alemán was blamed for handing out favors to his political intimates; some of these material concessions included lands taken from the Palomas Land and Cattle Company.[26]

[22] Ibid., p. 10.
[23] Ibid.
[24] IV Censo agrícola y ganadero, 1960, p. xviii.
[25] Ibid.
[26] Marte R. Gómez, La reforma agraria en las filas villistas, años 1913 a 1915 y 1920, p. 21: Lister and Lister, Chihuahua, p. 280.

Another foreign-owned cattle operation that received continual attention from various Mexican regimes was the Babícora Ranch of William Randolph Hearst. Beginning in the 1920's, various governments attempted to expropriate the lands. In 1953 the Mexican government and the Hearst interests settled their dispute; the government of Ruiz Cortínez paid Hearst $2.5 million for the property. In 1954 the Mexican government divided 50,000 hectares into twenty-hectare plots for the purpose of forming agricultural colonies.[27]

The need for additional grazing lands remained critical. The Banco Nacional indicated that between 1940 and 1955 Mexican cattle herds increased from 11.5 million to 14.9 million head. Thus, a reduction occurred in grazing land per head. In 1940 each livestock unit possessed 11.89 acres (approximately 4.6 hectares); in 1950 this dropped to 11.25 acres (approximately 4.5 hectares); and by 1955 the figure had declined drastically to 8.77 acres (3.55 hectares). Mexico was thus forced to search for a more scientific method of stock-raising than year-round pasturage.[28]

The increase in Mexican cattle between 1946 and 1960 resulted in large measure from breed improvement projects and from the replacement of cattle lost to foot-and-mouth disease. In 1946, for example, the state of Chihuahua alone imported 2,000 breeding animals, divided almost equally between bulls and cows. The onset of aftosa reduced importations, but these increased soon after 1952. In 1955, Chihuahua imported over 2,000 seed bulls; in 1957, 780 seed bulls and 882 brood cows.[29]

Efforts at breed improvement of Mexican cattle had started in the late nineteenth century, when large landholders, responding to an export market in the United States, began to cross Hereford and Shorthorn bulls with criollo cattle. By 1930 over 50 percent of the cattle in northern Mexico, compared with 17 percent in 1910, were Herefords or Hereford crosses, yielding a highly satisfactory crossbred beef animal.[30] By 1950 over half the Mexican cattle pro-

[27] Lister and Lister, *Chihuahua*, pp. 279–280.
[28] Banco Nacional de México, "Some Aspects of Mexican Stock Raising," Exámen de la Situación Económica de México, vol. 32, pp. 12–13.
[29] Alfonso Reina Celaya, *La industria de la carne en México*, p. 125.
[30] "El ganado vacuno," *Monografías comerciales: Boletín mensual de la dirección rural* 227 (April, 1945), 207.

duction was centered in the north and was destined for slaughter. This beef, composed of pure beef breeds or crosses of these, attested to the increasing quality of Mexican beef cattle.[31]

Various drastic measures combined to improve the Mexican cattle industry between 1940 and 1960. Aftosa, of course, eliminated large numbers of cattle through the slaughter programs. In addition, the demands of the export market forced northern cattlemen especially to work constantly for breed improvement. These pressures for improvement resulted in the importation both of blooded stock and of semen for the artificial insemination program established during the aftosa outbreak. Additionally, federal credit lines became available to cattlemen seeking loans to improve their beef and dairy cattle.[32]

The Mexican government, however, continued to maintain a commitment to the agrarian ideals of the Revolution. Ejidatarios and campesinos received almost four thousand bulls from the government at no cost because they could not otherwise afford to improve their livestock.[33] Subsequently, the government provided financial aid to keep this segment of the Mexican agricultural population in the cattle business while paying less attention to the northern ranchers who generated millions in export income.

In fact, the cattle business in Mexico continued to be an expensive operation that required the use of extensive acreage for pasturage. Alanís Patiño estimated that in Chihuahua in 1947 a typical ranch operation required 30,000 hectares to accommodate 2,900 head of stock. These would break down in the following way: 2,000 brood cows, 800 yearlings and two-year-olds, and 100 seed bulls. The total investment in land, horses, equipment, and cattle amounted to approximately 750,000 pesos. Annual costs for operation came to almost 376,000 pesos and had an annual return of 170,000 pesos, or 23 percent. These figures applied to the use of blooded stock. An outfit that utilized criollo cattle could expect a return of only 16 percent.[34]

[31] Emilio Alanís Patiño, "La industria de la carne en México," *Problemas agrícolas e industriales de México* 4 (July–September, 1952), p. 243.

[32] Banco Nacional, "Aspects of Stock Raising," p. 13.

[33] Reina Celaya, *La industria de la carne*, p. 143.

[34] Alanís Patiño, "La industria de la carne," p. 243.

Dominating the entire cattle industry was an institutional bureaucracy that had received its impetus under Cárdenas and continued to grow into the 1950's. In August, 1950, there existed 610 local uniones ganaderas; these in turn were affiliated with 28 regional groups. The regional groups paid allegiance to the Confederación Nacional Ganadera, headquartered in Mexico City and operating under the aegis of the federal government.[35]

The federal government also involved itself in the cattle industry through the extension of financial credit for the improvement of the cattle industry. Although still aimed principally at the ejidatario and the campesino, relatively easy federal credit did become available to the cattleman in Mexico. In 1949, when the aftosa epidemic in Mexico reached its high point, private banks in Mexico controlled 74.8 million pesos for the improvement of the cattle industry. In that year the Banco Nacional de Crédito Agrícola y Ganadero loaned only 4 million pesos to aid the recovery of the cattle industry. Mexican cattlemen found it more feasible to approach banks in the United States Southwest for loans; these banks charged only 6 percent interest compared with 10 percent imposed by the Banco Nacional.[36]

An ancillary source of fiscal credit for cattle production came from the Nacional Financiera (National Financier), a government agency that in the 1940's and 1950's provided loans for meat-packing plants and granted tax cuts for ten years to packers who would form new companies. In this way the government hoped to extend relief and some control to the marketing of Mexican cattle.[37]

Fickle weather also helped improve the Mexican cattle industry. In 1956 drought plagued the United States Southwest. The USDA arranged a loan through the Export-Import Bank to Mexico for $5 million. Mexico in turn loaned this money to cattlemen for the purchase of breeding stock from the drought-plagued Southwest. North Mexican cattlemen, however, obtained money primarily from the Banco Nacional de Crédito Agrícola y Ganadero.[38]

[35] Ibid., p. 245.

[36] Ibid.; Banco Nacional de Crédito Agrícola y Ganadero, *Veinticinco años del Banco Nacional de Crédito Agrícola y Ganadero*, pp. 30–31.

[37] Banco Nacional, "Aspects of Stock Raising," p. 12.

[38] USDA Press Release, October 31, 1956, Agricultural History Branch Files; Brandenburg, *Modern Mexico*, p. 251.

Between 1946 and 1960 the Mexican cattle industry firmly established itself as an important segment of the national economy. It became the sixth most important economic enterprise in the nation, generating 343.3 million pesos, or 5.05 percent of the gross national product, in 1939. By 1948, despite the aftosa outbreak, cattle accounted for almost 1.4 billion pesos, nearly 4.5 percent of the gross national product. The figures indicate a gross increase but also a slight decline in total economic impact.[39]

Aftosa, a forced change in governmental direction, and persistent though contradictory commitments to agrarian reform and increased production both hampered and aided the cattle industry. Three major factors stimulated growth: first, the diet of the Mexican population increasingly came to include beef as a more than occasional component; second, Mexican cattle producers possessed increased economic capacity to meet demand; finally, international commerce promoted increased production and improvement of the cattle industry—a major export market asked for and received an improved product.[40] These trends would continue into the 1960's and 1970's.

[39] Reina Celaya, *La industria de la carne*, pp. 152–153.
[40] Alanís Patiño, "La industria de la carne," p. 236.

6. An Industry Restored, 1960–1975

THE years between 1946 and 1960 were a period of adjustment to peacetime demands for beef, of recuperation from the trauma of endemic livestock disease, and of increasing governmental institutionalization of the cattle industry. Especially in northern Mexico, cattlemen retained a traditional approach while at the same time adapting to the new technology, improved techniques of husbandry, and increasing government involvement.

The threat of expropriation and the division of cattle pastures into ejidos continued to loom on the cattleman's horizon in Mexico. The complex nexus of land laws, both state and federal, was subject to amendment if agrarian authorities could justify the social utility of such changes. High government functionaries, whether truly committed or not, found themselves accepting the idea of increased ejido development, even for the cattle industry and in spite of the questionable efficiency of ejido production. In Chihuahua, for example, Governor Oscar Flores, former head of CMAPEFA under Alemán, attempted to advocate a middle-of-the-road course. According to Flores, extensive holdings were inefficient. His own cattle operation in 1965 approached thirty thousand hectares. In Flores' view, ejidos would provide a better basis for the production of better cattle! "Cattle production will increase in Chihuahua. Not in number, but in weight and quality."[1]

Cattlemen were constantly required to justify their large holdings. Increased ejido cattle productivity became the watchword for the agricultural sector. By law, cattlemen contributed 2 percent of their annual calf crop to the ejidos; in this way they could en-

[1] Charles R. Koch, "Beef below the Border," *Farm Quarterly* 24 (Summer, 1969), p. 49.

sure that for another year the government would leave their lands intact. In traditional manner, however, the *mordida* often helped the more influential cattlemen avoid the 2 percent levy.[2]

Two concerns about land plagued cattlemen in northern Mexico after 1960. The first was the status of the decrees of unaffectability of the 1940's; most of them were due to expire in 1965 and few if any were renewed. The expiration of these decrees left the land subject to expropriation. Nevertheless, the government recognized the necessity for larger landholdings in the north. In 1971 it attempted again to clarify what was a legitimate landholding for the purposes of a pastoral industry. Again it reaffirmed its commitment to the idea that land capable of supporting 500 head of stock without area definition was an optimum size for a cattle operation.[3]

Still, with optimum number of cattle giving definition to the ideal ranch, cattlemen continued to worry about the possibility of future expropriation of lands that had been improved through irrigation, fertilizer, and increased mechanization. With modernized methods, production could be intensified, but how would that affect the size of a cattleman's holding after the acreage had been improved? Would the government seek to reduce a holding because technological advances had been made upon it? Governmental response came in the Federal Land Reform Law of 1971, which attempted to clarify the ambiguities in existing land legislation. The law categorically declared that unaffected landholdings improved through new technology would not be subject to expropriation as a result of the improvements. The United Nations Economic Commission for Latin America in 1975 calculated, upon the basis of a typical cattle operation in Sonora, that one vaquero could manage cattle in an area of approximately 6,000 hectares, or approximately one cow-calf unit per 148 acres. The revised agrarian codes recognized that cattle production in the north could be determined only by an optimum number of animals, not by an arbitrary quantity of land. This land constituted the major investment for cattlemen, around 70 percent of the total.[4]

[2] Ibid., p. 47.

[3] United Nations Comisión Económica para América Latina (CEPAL), *La industria de la carne de ganado bovino en México*, p. 17.

[4] Ibid., pp. 17, 49–50.

No doubt exists that improved cattle characterized Mexico after 1955. Mexican officials claimed that each administration from Carranza through Cárdenas had attempted to improve the Mexican cattle industry and to augment production. Government efforts promoted the importation of blooded breeding stock for the purpose of upgrading Mexican cattle. Herefords provided the predominant genetic pool for the outcrosses to criollo stock. Initially, importers of blooded stock enjoyed a 50 percent discount on the national railways as a means of inducing increased importation of breeding animals. Beginning with Cárdenas, regional centers were established where seed bulls would service the cattle of the ejidatarios. This proved a cumbersome arrangement, for the cows had to be brought to the center for servicing. In the 1950's, as a result of the aftosa outbreak, artificial insemination centers were established. Seed bulls were brought into Mexico from the United States in order to provide greater genetic variety for livestock improvement. By 1970 the Mexican government saw the cattle industry as improving both qualitatively and quantitatively. Its industrial potential had increased in three aspects: ejidal, ranchera (small private holdings), and industrial or extensive production of livestock.[5]

Government officials in Mexico argued that the key to the intensive development of the cattle industry lay in the exchange program between the Ministry of Agriculture and Husbandry and the ejidatarios. The program involved the loan of a bull to an ejido, which in turn paid an insurance premium of 110 pesos. Should the bull die, the secretariat would then be reimbursed for the bull and would provide yet another bull for that particular ejido. Government plans called for wide distribution of these seed bulls in order to increase ejido production and to upgrade the cattle industry.[6]

Between 1960 and 1970, cattlemen in Chihuahua increasingly aimed their production toward the United States. Using improved knowledge of range management and agricultural technology, these cattlemen steadily increased their exports to United States markets

---

[5] "Plan para el mejoramiento genético mediante el canje de bovinos corrientes por sementales de raza pura" (Manuscript supplied by the Dirección General de Ganadería, April, 1972).

[6] Ibid.

in the Southwest. They based their accelerated production on the drought-resistant black grama grass that serves as the basis of forage on t e plateau running from Mexico City to Ciudad Juárez.

Paradoxically, however, innovations in the production of beef cattle in the north failed to sweep away many of the traditional approaches of the people who worked the stock on a daily basis. Chihuahua vaqueros remained staunch traditionalists. They lived in *jacales* (huts), continued to use horses for working cattle, and maintained other practices characteristic of a pastoral culture. The *ganaderos* (cattlemen), however, increasingly adopted the trappings of their Southwestern counterparts. Cowboy boots, Stetsons, and pickup trucks abound in the Chihuahua plains.[7]

The simultaneous phenomena of cultural persistence and adaptation to a modern lifestyle typified the changes that came to the norteño cattle industry during the 1960's. Limitations on the size of land holdings forced improvement of Chihuahua cattle through a more intensive approach to cattle raising. Wells, stock tanks, improved breeding programs, and supplemental feeds testified to modernization, while the persistence of traditional values attested to the essentially conservative nature of the cattle industry. In terms of breed improvement, in the late 1960's Chihuahua cattle showed a 65 percent Hereford population, while Aberdeen Anguses composed only 3 percent of the total cattle population and Zebus merely 0.5 percent. Criollo cattle, though showing marked Hereford influence, remained at about 31.5 percent in 1966.[8]

The government of Chihuahua recognized that the cattle industry was essential to the economy of the state. Range experiment stations run by the state government conducted experiments in arid-land forage in order to improve ranges. The provincial university in Chihuahua City maintained a school of animal husbandry "to train her young men for this old and honored profession."[9]

Other states in northern Mexico also pride themselves on cattle production, but none possess the nearly atavistic worship of the industry that the *chihuahuenses* demonstrate. In 1960 the Unión

[7] Florence C. Lister and Robert H. Lister, *Chihuahua: Storehouse of Storms*, p. 283.
[8] Ibid., p. 284.
[9] Ibid., p. 285.

Regional Ganadera of Chihuahua held four livestock expositions to celebrate the fiftieth anniversary of the Mexican Revolution. In competition with cattle from Durango, Estado de México, Chiapas, Aguascalientes, Nuevo León, Sinaloa, Coahuila, and Sonora, Chihuahua cattlemen won three championships and seven first places. In 1966 the membership of the twenty-seven local groups of the Unión Regional Ganadera had risen to 4,500. The Unión Regional maintained 139 radio transmitters in outlying ranches, worked at the eradication of toxic plants, and encouraged stock improvement through artificial insemination.[10]

Upgrading of Mexican beef cattle resulted from efforts by both government and private parties. By the mid-1960's northern ranchers showed marked improvements in the quality of their beef stock. Throughout northern Mexico, private and public enterprises provided high-grade genetic pools for breed improvement. In Coahuila excellent centers for Charolais cattle abounded; Chihuahua was dominated by Herefords and some Angus; Sonora ran mixed breeds on irrigated pastures. Some of the newer breeds—Brangus, Beefmasters, and various other crosses—also increased in the area. Interest in breed improvement led the federal government in the early 1970's to begin a program at the experiment station at La Campana. Under the direction of the Instituto Nacional de Investigaciones Pecuarias (formerly the Direccion General de Investigaciones Pecuarias), the station at La Campana imported selected breeding stock from twenty-four exotic breeds. These animals, such as Simmental and Maine-Anjou, continue to be tested for their adaptability to the harsh Chihuahua environment. In this way, the genetic pool of northern Mexico's cattle herds has been increasingly diversified.[11]

In 1960, imports of breeding cattle and dairy stock for central Mexico continued to increase: in that year, Mexico imported a total of nearly six thousand head of registered stock with a value of over 20 million pesos; at the same time, in order to upgrade commercial herds, she imported over fourteen thousand head of unregistered breeding animals valued at 47.5 million pesos. By 1970 the number

[10] Ibid.
[11] Koch, "Beef below the Border," p. 45; CEPAL, *La industria de la carne*, pp. 33–34.

of imported registered breeding stock had declined to slightly below three thousand head worth 15.1 million pesos.[12]

Throughout the 1960's, Mexico showed a general surplus of agricultural products except in cattle production. Increased demands for beef on the table increased the pressure on cattlemen to send more beef animals to urban areas, especially to Mexico City. Mexican export restrictions required cattlemen to send 20 head of cattle to Mexico City at a government-fixed price for every 100 exported to the United States. It proved to be a costly program to cattlemen; most preferred to pay a subsidy rather than deliver the 20 head per 100 shipped north. In Sonora the subsidy was forty pesos per head; in Chihuahua, thirty.[13]

Thus, cattle exports to the United States continued to increase. In 1960 over 318,000 feeder cattle weighing between 100 and 250 kilograms each entered the United States; heavier stock (over 250 kilograms) numbered more than 76,000. In the next year, 424,000 head of feeders with a value of almost 192 million pesos entered the United States; heavier, finished slaughter cattle exceeded 121,000 head and was worth approximately 102 million pesos. In 1962 cattle exports from Mexico increased radically—in all classes, almost 740,000 head—and dropped sharply in 1963 and 1964.[14]

Between 1965 and 1970, Mexican cattlemen continued to increase the number of livestock exported to the United States market. In 1965 feeders exported to the United States approached 482,000; in 1968, almost 688,000, an increase of almost 50 percent, or nearly 307 million pesos. In 1969 the figure went even higher (over 817,000 head) and in 1970 levelled off to nearly 788,000.[15] Surprisingly, the quota system used by the Mexican government to assure that Mexico City received a ready supply of beef failed from its inception. In 1968, for example, the secretary of agriculture and

[12] *Anuario estadístico de comercio exterior*, 1960, p. 14; *Anuario estadístico*, 1965, p. 1; *Anuario estadístico*, 1970, p. 3.

[13] Koch, "Beef below the Border," p. 47; USDA Press Release, June 26, 1968, Agricultural History Branch Files, U.S. Department of Agriculture, Washington, D.C.

[14] *Anuario estadístico*, 1960–1962 and 1964, pp. 560 and 683, respectively.

[15] *Anuario estadístico*, 1965, 1968, and 1970, pp. 545, 613, and 621, respectively.

husbandry determined that the export quota for Mexican cattle should be 636,000 head of all classes.[16]

Although Mexican cattlemen in the decade 1960–1970 willingly shipped as many cattle as the United States could accommodate, sanitary restrictions by both countries curbed unlimited exportation. By Mexican law, only cattle from the twelve northern states could be shipped to the United States. The United States, moreover, would accept cattle from only eight of these—Tamaulipas, Nuevo León, Chihuahua, Coahuila, Sonora, Baja California, Durango, and Zacatecas—largely because they lie north of the tick line (the line south of which Mexican cattle were considered contaminated with fever ticks and thus potential vectors for spreading disease to United States livestock). Mexican cattlemen could not export breeding age stock, either bulls or cows; these had to stay on their home ranges in order to produce market animals to feed the growing population in Mexico City.[17]

Adding to the export difficulties of Mexican cattlemen is the limitation of space at United States ports of entry. The uniones ganaderas distribute the quotas to members once the figures have been determined by the government. Individual cattlemen apply directly to their local unión ganadera for a permit and are limited to shipping cattle no older than two years of age. First, however, they must check to see if space is available at the holding pens near the border. The Unión Regional Ganadera de Chihuahua, for example, maintains corrals for 9,000 head of cattle in Ciudad Juárez. During the peaks of the shipping season—September through December and again in April—space becomes precious. The permit is valid for only ten days after issue, so that cattlemen are forced to hustle for available space until their cattle are allowed across the border.[18]

The complexities of getting the cattle across the border are increased by the cost of processing the animals from one country to the other. Calculations in 1965 revealed that the cost to a Mexican rancher was approximately $0.07 per pound. Sonora's fees

16 Koch, "Beef below the Border," p. 46.
17 Ibid., pp. 45, 46.
18 Ibid., p. 46.

are typical: a state tax of 87.50 pesos per head and a cost of 9.30 pesos per head for a bill of sale boosted the costs to nearly 100 pesos or $8.00 as of 1965. In addition, Mexico charged an export tax of 7 centavos per pound; the United States imposed an import duty of $0.025 per pound on animals weighing between 200 and 700 pounds; heavier animals paid $0.015 per pound. Finally, a brokerage fee of $0.25 per head appeared on the bill.[19] Thus, the cost at the border to the Mexican cattleman in 1965 was approximately 752 pesos or a little over $60.00 for a 700-pound feeder steer.

Foot-and-mouth disease no longer posed a major problem for the Mexican cattle industry. Vigilance at the Dirección General de Investigaciones Pecuarias through the investigation of any outbreaks of vesicular disease maintained a ready control over suspected reappearances of aftosa or confirmed diagnoses of vesicular exanthema in hogs and vesicular stomatitis in cattle and horses. The Dirección General de Investigaciones Pecuarias expanded its investigatory activities at its headquarters in Palo Alto. One of the most serious cattle plagues to which it addressed itself was *derriengue,* or paralytic rabies, in both beef and dairy cattle. The persistence of this disease in Mexico, transmitted to livestock by vampire bats, caused losses of up to 130 million pesos per year.[20] Other diseases, such as piroplasmosis, hemoragghic septicemia, and screwworm, brought the loss to billions of pesos.[21]

Screwworm posed a serious problem in United States–Mexican relations, for it was endemic in both the United States and Mexico and required a joint effort for its eradication.

Screwworms, the larvae of the screwworm fly, make all warm-blooded animals, including man, a target. The female lays her eggs—up to four hundred at a time—in even the most minute lesions. The eggs hatch within twelve to twenty-four hours after deposit, become larvae in five to seven days, and begin feeding on healthy tissue. Larval and pupal stages conclude seven to ten days

[19] Ibid., p. 47.

[20] "Las enfermedades de los animales domésticos como factor limitante en la producción pecuaria en México" (Manuscript supplied by the Dirección General de Sanidad Animal, Secretaría de Agricultura y Ganadería, April, 1972).

[21] Secretaría de Agricultura y Ganadería, *Cría y explotación del ganado bovino.*

after hatching, the adult fly is born, and the life cycle begins again.[22] Screwworms pose a threat because the open wounds upon which the larvae feed become increasingly susceptible to secondary infections through an increase in the size of the wound and the deep burrowing that occurs. Screwworms are generally confined to tropical and semitropical areas; mild, moist winters contribute significantly to the survival of larvae and flies. Research has indicated that the migratory capacity of the adult flies can range up to 180 miles.

Screwworm in the United States has persisted since the early nineteenth century. Infestations ranged from the Southwest to the Southeast, visiting severe damage on both livestock and human populations. Screwworm also affected cattle in Mexico. In the United States, programs were initiated in both the Southeast and the Southwest in 1958 and 1959 respectively. By the end of 1959, the Southeast was free of screwworm. The program cost $11 million but averted over $20 million in losses. The United States Southwest, however, presented some additional problems. There, the principal obstacle to effective screwworm control was the extent of the wintering areas of the adult fly. Two thousand miles of contiguous border made it appreciably easier for flies from Mexico to reinfest clean areas in the United States Southwest.

In February, 1962, Secretary of Agriculture Orville Freeman announced a massive campaign to eradicate screwworm. He declared that it would be a combined effort between the Agricultural Research Service, the Southwest Animal Health Research Foundation (composed of cattlemen), and the Texas Animal Health Commission, and would utilize sterile fly techniques that had worked successfully in the Southeast.[23] State and federal authorities and representatives of the livestock industry contributed large sums to the campaign to eradicate screwworm; the Southwest Animal Research Foundation also contributed $4.5 million toward eradication. In June, 1962, Vice-president Lyndon B. Johnson dedicated new re-

[22] The bulk of information on screwworm is derived from USDA Animal and Plant Health Inspection Service, *Progress in Screwworm Eradication*. Unless otherwise indicated, all information comes from this source.
[23] USDA Press Release, February 13, 1962, Agricultural History Branch Files.

search facilities at Mission, Texas, devoted to screwworm eradication. Nearby Moore Air Force Base provided a plant for the production of sterile flies with which the United States Southwest and northern Mexico would be bombarded. Mexican dignitaries attended the dedication ceremony.[24]

Maintenance of an effective program required rancher cooperation. Livestock producers were asked to check their animals regularly, collect samples of suspicious larvae, and treat wounds that would provide hatching grounds for screwworm eggs.

The initial program enjoyed almost total success. By September, 1963, Mexico and the United States were cooperating effectively in the creation of a barrier zone along the Rio Grande. The barrier zone proved to be the most effective means of controlling the spread of screwworm fly. Established in order to reduce reinfestations, it required maintenance and vigilance. Constant surveillance continued, samples were collected, and sterile flies continued to be introduced into the area in order to prevent fly reproduction. In 1964, wintering screwworm fly populations in the southwestern United States were effectively eradicated, and by the end of 1966, the last screwworm populations had been eliminated in Arizona and California.

The menace was not wholly eradicated in 1966. United States and Mexican representatives in Mexico City conferred regarding screwworm control. It was noted that the weather in northern Mexico and in the Southwest was not cold enough to eradicate fly populations. The Confederación Nacional Ganadera promised to contribute financially to the campaign against screwworm if funds were needed.[25]

Once again Mexico and the United States joined in a common effort to eradicate a common livestock malady. Under a cooperative agreement signed in 1966, scientists at the Dirección General de Investigaciones Pecuarias undertook study of the physiology, behavior, and other characteristics of the screwworm fly. Funding came in large part from the USDA.[26]

[24] USDA Press Release, June 12, 1962, Agricultural History Branch Files.

[25] USDA Press Releases, March 15 and March 24, 1966, Agricultural History Branch Files.

[26] USDA Press Release, August 4, 1966, Agricultural History Branch Files.

While control was being effected, total eradication still remained to be achieved. Budgetary reductions cut the number of sterile flies that could be released into the area. Although long screwworm-free periods existed, nearly 10,000 cases were reported in the United States in 1968. Northern Mexico experienced nearly 20,000 cases of infestation; the release of millions of sterile flies into the area averted a major outbreak. By late 1969, screwworm cases had declined radically.[27] The year 1970 marked the lowest point for screwworm cases: only 153 confirmed cases occurred in the United States; Mexico reported over 4,000 in 1970 compared with almost double that figure in 1969. During 1970 the plant in Mission, Texas, produced 6.94 billion sterile flies that were released through Mexico and the United States Southwest.[28]

Unfortunately, the barrier zone failed to stop the infestations. By mid-February, 1971, screwworm cases appeared in Hidalgo County, Texas, as well as in northern Mexico. The USDA noted that Mexican cases were closer to the border than they had been in the past. The United States Congress acted quickly. A bill introduced in the Senate amended the original 1947 legislation that enabled cooperation between the United States and Mexico in foot-and-mouth disease control; the new legislation, promoted in large part by Senator John Tower of Texas, allowed the secretary of agriculture to cooperate with Mexican authorities in the control of all communicable animal diseases.[29]

Mexico and the United States signed an agreement on August 28, 1972, for the establishment of a Mexican–United States Commission on Screwworm Eradication. The Mexican program, headquartered in Mexico City, receives 80 percent of its funding from the United States. Each week 500 million sterile flies come from laboratories in Tuxtla Gutiérrez on the Isthmus of Tehuántepec for release in afflicted areas. Mexican eradication was projected for about mid-1979. In addition, once successful screwworm eradica-

[27] USDA Press Releases, December 26, 1968, January 14, July 30, and October 21, 1969, Agricultural History Branch Files.

[28] USDA Press Release, January 19, 1971, Agricultural History Branch Files.

[29] USDA Press Release, February 19, 1971, Agricultural History Branch Files; *Congressional Record*, August 2 and October 6, 1971.

tion had occurred north of the Isthmus of Tehuántepec, a new barrier zone was to be established at approximately 20 percent of the cost of maintaining the larger zone in the north.

The transfer of scientific technology to Mexico for screwworm eradication represents one of the unheralded achievements of international cooperation. Fly sterilization ultimately proved to be cheaper and more effective than insecticide spraying in the eradication of screwworm. The process, refined in Mission, Texas, requires the collection of eggs from a fertile fly colony. The larvae hatch, mature, and begin pupation. At this point they are exposed to 7,000 roentgens of gamma radiation derived from Cesium-137. Male flies are thus effectively sterilized; although they can indulge their libidos, they cannot reproduce. Mating instincts are satisfied, but the sterilized males cannot fertilize the eggs.

Traditional relationships and the excellent system of north-south transportation in Mexico aided the north Mexican cattle industry in the delivery of feeder stock to the United States. With over 34 percent of the cattle in the nation, norteño cattlemen found the competitive prices offered by United States buyers consistently higher than the fixed prices offered in Mexico City. Thus, they continued to ship increasing quantities of stock into the United States.[30]

Live cattle were not the only products aimed at buyers in the southwestern United States. Fresh meat also had a ready market along the border. As a result, slaughterhouses in northern Mexico were constructed that adhered to rigorous inspection standards for the processing of meat that could then be transported across the international boundary. These plants, designated Tipo de Inspección Federal (Federal Inspection Type), shipped thousands of pounds of meat to the United States.[31]

Increased shipments of livestock to the United States and increased production on northern ranges in Mexico still faced the nearly overwhelming problems of minimal-quality pasturage. Despite some experimentation with different, hardier grasses, only 3 percent of the pastureland in the north could be classified as excel-

[30] CEPAL, *La industria de la carne*, pp. 28–29.
[31] Ibid., pp. 47–48.

lent; approximately 70 percent ranged from poor to average. In addition, problems of fertility associated with improper diet complicated the ability of Mexican cattlemen to produce at maximum capacity despite the landholdings available to them. Deficient nutrition made itself evident in the birth rates in Mexican brood cows, which varied from 40 to 65 percent. Moreover, because lack of controlled management of cattle herds is the rule rather than the exception, breeding tends to be indiscriminate, so that many of the resulting issue are unfit as breeders and should be culled; yet, substandard females are kept on and in turn produce substandard calves, continuing the downward cycle. Forty to fifty percent of the yearlings are probably unfit for reproduction because of poor conformation, genetic defect, or a general incapacity to produce a meatier carcass.[32]

If the larger individual cattle operations face problems, the few cattle ejidos in northern Mexico have even greater difficulties. Low-quality pastures—a common problem—coupled with a lack of administrative responsibility for pasture rotation produce substandard cattle. This in turn removes ejido cattle producers from the export market. Ejidatarios must then turn to other forms of production; scrub criollo cattle interbred with dairy stock form the basis of most ejido cattle herds in northern Mexico. Nevertheless, the dairy emphasis fails to give a high production standard to the cattle ejidos: cows on one ejido in Cananea, Sonora, produced an average of only four to six liters of milk per cow per day. Despite publicity given to cattle ejidos in the north, their production capacity remains low. Ejidatarios make few long-term investments. There is practically no capital investment for upgrading pastures, and little breed improvement despite the availability of government bulls.[33]

Mexican cattle production in the 1960's and into the mid-1970's continued the trends apparent in the immediate postwar period. After 1970, cattle exports to the United States levelled off at slightly over one-half million head with a value of about eighty million dollars per year. At the same time, the United States ex-

---

[32] Ibid., pp. 52–53.
[33] Ibid., pp. 63–66.

ported breeding stock to Mexico carrying an average value of over twenty million dollars per year.[34] Thus, the mutual dependency between cattlemen on both sides of the Rio Grande continued to grow. While more money was being spent in Mexico than in the United States for breeding stock, United States cattlemen could realize a greater return on their investments through the utilization of high-grade Mexican feeder cattle.

Increased government involvement in the cattle industry of northern Mexico was often circumvented either through graft or through loopholes in the various regulations affecting production. On the positive side, the increased efforts by both the public and private sectors indicated that the cattle industry remained important in Mexico.

Mexican officials maintained their commitment to the ejido as the principal source of agricultural production. As of 1975, United Nations findings indicated that the few cattle ejidos in northern Mexico were not competitive in the export market that characterizes livestock activity in that area. Failure to accompany commitment to an ideal with practical education programs left the ejido producers on the margins of both dairy and beef production.

In the area of livestock disease control, the efforts of Mexico and the United States in screwworm eradication found their roots in the anti-aftosa campaign of the 1940's and early 1950's. Both countries, impelled by a benevolent self-interest, recognized the necessity of cooperation and acted accordingly. Accordingly, screwworm, one of the most persistent and insidious of livestock afflictions, is nearing extinction. A foundation had been laid; both countries used it effectively.

[34] USDA, *Computer Printout Tables by the Foreign Demand and Competition Divisions of the Economics, Statistics, and Cooperative Service*, January 31, 1979.

7. A Summing Up

Mexico nurtured her cattle industry for four hundred years before a massive revolution in the twentieth century left it devastated. Mexican cattle met demands for increasing amounts of beef in the United States diet at a time when the urban centers of the United States were growing. Mexico responded to the demands by upgrading beef quality and producing almost exclusively for the northern market.

But the Revolution changed all that. Ten years of conflict nearly annihilated a viable industry. Modern pressures forced Mexico to change its direction. Unionization, democratization, equitable distribution of land, and generalized egalitarianism forced those cattlemen who had survived the Revolution of 1910–1920 into a defensive posture; they were thrust into the role of societal pariahs and depicted as feudal exploiters. Regardless of the merits and disadvantages of the large haciendas of northern Mexico, the fact remains that those people who were best equipped to rebuild a vital sector of the agricultural economy were either shunned or harassed by successive governments responding to different pressures.

The incorporation of revolutionary promises into the Constitution of 1917 and the contradictory pressures that beset the Mexican government after 1920 militated against heavy investments in the rebuilding of the cattle industry. An agrarian commitment dominated the thinking of Mexican political leaders. The promise of land redistribution intoxicated the landless, uneducated peasants, who after 1920 began to demand that the government fulfill its revolutionary promises. Symbolic expropriations occurred, most notably that of the huge estates of Luis Terrazas, who in the popular view represented the old order, the regime that had been headed by Porfirio Díaz. For a while expropriation of the Terrazas estates mollified agrarista pressures. The restoration of foreign-owned lands to Mexicans had been a principal tenet of the Revolution. Expropriations of foreign-, principally United States–owned, haciendas in northern Mexico thus fulfilled a revolutionary promise. The nationalization of some, though not all, foreign haciendas superficially delivered on another and made additional land available for redistribution. Mexican cattlemen, both foreign and domestic, felt reluctant to expend huge sums of money rebuilding haciendas, buying new cattle, and refurbishing facilities merely to have them summarily expropriated by a fickle and seemingly whimsical government. Consequently the cattle industry in Mexico merely survived during the 1920's and 1930's. Cattlemen held their collective breaths hoping that their lands might not be expropriated.

Agrarian reform prevented not only direct investment in the cattle industry but also the development of ancillary enterprises. The activity most neglected was the production of supplementary feeds, principally cereals: arable lands were kept out of grain production, and the cattle industry continued to rely almost exclusively on year-round forage for the feeding of livestock. Without feed supplements, Mexico could not finish livestock as slaughter cattle; as a direct result Mexico became a supplier of feeder stock for the United States.[1] This development in turn created a dependency that was regarded with some apprehension by Mexicans and their government.

Like so many other aspects of Mexican life, the cattle industry eventually succumbed to institutionalization. Pressures on his government for some guarantees to the cattle industry led Lázaro Cárdenas to grant concessions. His most significant contribution was the formation of the uniones regionales ganaderas that culminated in the Confederación Nacional Ganadera. This, along with other programs orchestrated by the federal government, facilitated the imposition of controls by the government in Mexico City. Export quotas were determined by the secretary of agriculture and

---

[1] Floyd E. Davis and George J. Dietz, *Beef Cattle in Northern Mexico and Probable Exports to the United States*, p. 19.

husbandry and distributed by the uniones regionales. The establishment of ceilings on beef prices in Mexico City also reflected increased government control. The provisions for the supplying of calves to northern ejidos by norteño cattlemen bespoke the adherence of the central authority to an ejido ideal.

Mexico continues to play an important role in the cattle industry of the United States. The annual export of between 500,000 and 950,000 head of feeder stock to the United States during the last two decades clearly attests to the increasing demand for beef in the United States. Yet, as early as 1965, some warnings were being sounded. How much longer could Mexico continue to provide one of the last few sources of good light feeder calves? Increases in Mexico's standard of living led to demands for more beef on Mexican tables. Mexico, it was surmised, might "find that it can ill afford the luxury of exporting cattle."[2]

Rugged conditions in northern Mexico strengthened the animals sent to the United States. These feeder calves were described as hardier, healthier, and hungrier than stock north of the Rio Grande. Although considerable red tape hindered the north Mexican cattleman, he found that he could still get his best calves to the United States market.[3]

Mutual dependency characterized the relations of the United States and Mexico with regard to the importation of breeding stock and the control of livestock diseases. Mexico provided a ready market for surplus breeding cattle from the United States. Mexican cattlemen as well as the Mexican government sought to improve the quality of Mexican cattle. As a result, Mexican officials were faced with a dilemma: although they sought to improve the quality of cattle in Mexico generally, they disliked their dependency on the United States as a supplier of breeding stock. Occasional imports from other supplier nations, principally in South America, failed to produce the quality of animal needed to improve the general genetic pool of Mexican cattle. Consequently, Mexico has continued to rely on the United States as a principal source of breeding stock.

[2] Charles R. Koch, "Beef below the Border," *Farm Quarterly* 24 (Summer, 1969), p. 45.
[3] Ibid., p. 46.

Overall, the Mexican cattle industry has contributed approximately 35 percent of the gross agricultural production in Mexico. The export market to the United States has contributed greatly to the increased demands for revenue in northern Mexico.[4]

With regard to livestock disease control, both countries have a common interest in protecting their tremendous investments in their respective cattle industries. The major cattle-producing areas of the two countries share a border of nearly 2,000 miles. As a result, when foot-and-mouth disease, tick fever, and screwworm became threats, both governments cooperated in the control and eradication of these maladies. Luckily, the extreme xenophobia of the early Revolution had abated by 1945, and the Mexican government found that cooperation was not so onerous. At the same time, United States representatives found sophisticated scientists in Mexico working on livestock disease problems, scientists whose contributions to veterinary medicine would make any nation proud. As a consequence, cooperation has persisted since the outbreak of various diseases. The maintenance of joint commissions and joint research efforts serve as testimony to the unifying nature of the cattle industry in both countries.

Finally, the distinctive cultures produced in the cattle country of both the United States and Mexico possess more similarities than differences. Traditional values based on individual endeavor, governmental decentralization, and a rough-and-ready individualism permeate northern Mexico and set it apart from the rest of the country. These qualities polarized the relations between cattlemen in northern Mexico and the central government. Resistance by cattlemen to governmental intervention grew from a desire to preserve what was rightfully theirs. But although cattlemen resisted the pressures, they were also forced to adapt in order to survive. Among the adaptations was a grudging acquiescence in the increasing involvement of government. Along the way they found that governmental involvement sometimes conferred benefits: livestock disease control, easily available credit, livestock experiment stations, and feed experimentation through the Instituto Nacional

---

[4] United Nations Comisíon Económica para América Latina, *La industria de la carne de ganado bovino en México*, pp. 9, 16.

de Investigaciones Pecuarias ultimately helped the larger cattle producers.

In many respects, the cattle industry offered an alternative to the communitarianism of the agraristas. Cattlemen knew that small parcels would not produce cattle in northern Mexico despite the government's persistent idea that marketable cattle could thrive on small ejido parcels.

In the broad spectrum of Mexican politics, traditional conservatives, among whom can be found northern cattlemen, view as anathema the land reform provisions of the Constitution of 1917. "They want the whole project overhauled, communal property ownership seriously qualified, and the Mexican countryside placed once again under the tutelage of rural land barons," writes Frank Brandenburg. He continues that "traditionalists of today are more likely to sustain their theories on the argument that Mexico's food supply shortages can only be overcome by replacing the inefficient communal *ejido* and small farm" with large, privately owned units based on mechanization and efficiency of production. Furthermore, "Whatever the economic soundness of this plan, it runs directly counter to some four decades of Revolutionary preaching on the social justice of collective land ownership, and any serious attempt to undo *ejidos* and subjugate the peasant . . . probably would provoke an impassioned uprising."[5]

Northern vaqueros have continued to live in much the same way that they always have. Adobe *jacales* serve as houses; horses still provide the major means of working transportation. However, the vaquero has not shared appreciably in the post-Revolutionary cattle boom. He might have a few scrawny head of cattle, or he might be a *contrabandista* if he lives near the border. He is described as a "leather-faced man of the wind and weather, solemn, taciturn, and dejected. More than that, he is disillusioned on realization that La Revolución, to which he contributed so much, has returned him nothing."[6]

Why has the vaquero received so little in return for his sacri-

[5] Frank Brandenburg, *The Making of Modern Mexico*, pp. 127–128.
[6] Florence C. Lister and Robert H. Lister, *Chihuahua: Storehouse of Storms*, p. 286.

fices? In part, his pre-1910 exploitation has continued in the post-Revolutionary period; traditional relationships between rancher and cowboy have persisted. But it is this same traditional posture, found in both rancher and worker, that has helped the beef cattle industry regain its major place in Mexican agriculture. The traditionalists have not only accepted the inevitability of centralization but also forced the central government to modify its approach to long-range changes in the beef cattle–producing north.

Has the Revolution failed to affect the north Mexican cattle industry? The most committed land reform advocates would probably answer in the affirmative. At most, the Revolution forced some divestiture of huge tracts of land through either expropriation or sale. Despite an ideological commitment to land reform, economic and political realities have tempered the attitudes of successive Mexican governments toward the northern beef industry. In so doing, they have recognized, in a way that ideology does not, the variations in the composition of the Mexican Republic.

Appendix: Statistical Tables

NOTE: All land measures are in hectares, monetary values in pesos, and weight in kilograms.

TABLE 1

Decrease in Mexican Cattle Population, 1902–1923

State	1902	1923	Total Loss
Sonora	260,732	69,350	191,382
Chihuahua	396,023	96,184	299,839
Durango	233,041	23,280	209,761
Nuevo León	123,388	61,572	61,816
Tamaulipas	178,271	29,800	148,471
Baja California	52,101	32,300	19,801

SOURCE: File no. 812.62/37, RG 59, NA.

TABLE 2

Cattle Imported to Mexico, 1920–1933

Country of Origin and Year	Quantity	Value
1921		
USA	24,745	1,794,110
Guatemala	2,772	173,278
Colombia	1,174	50,900
Total	29,379	2,110,708
1923		
USA	25,801	1,406,637
Colombia	23,796	1,474,761
Cuba	2,099	159,600
Total	52,722	3,151,730

TABLE 2 (cont'd.)

Country of Origin and Year	Quantity	Value
1924		
Colombia	8,821	387,490
USA	44,597	1,505,044
Brazil	85	16,083
Total	53,528	1,915,393
1925		
USA	81,825	3,444,405
Colombia	6,737	347,500
Other	1,162	48,567
Total	91,379	2,965,986
1926		
USA	20,793	1,034,875
British Honduras	8,858	90,307
Colombia	2,517	131,460
Total	33,011	1,383,214
1927		
USA	7,667	911,870
British Honduras	1,340	42,308
Holland	51	26,368
Total	9,074	982,472
1928		
USA	6,064	690,261
Guatemala	46	2,429
British Honduras	570	12,403
Total	7,609	843,210
1929		
USA	3,644	456,086
Total	4,754	707,014
1930		
USA	3,320	461,209
Total	4,095	551,781
1931		
USA (1931–1933)	2,187	254,383
Total	2,488	400,095
1932		
USA (1931–1933)	2,187	254,383
Total	4,170	369,831
1933		
USA (1931–1933)	2,187	254,383
Total	2,199	255,161

SOURCE: *Anuarios estadísticos de comercio exterior,* 1921–1933.

NOTE: Discrepancies between totals and numbers from individual countries derive from a statistically insignificant miscellaneous number of cattle imported from other countries.

TABLE 3

Cattle Exported from Mexico, 1920–1933

Destination and Year	Quantity	Value
1920		
USA	43,016	1,389,862
Peru	18	1,800
Spain	3	1,600
Total	43,037	1,403,262
1921		
USA	13,055	406,344
Guatemala	22	5,000
Total	13,077	411,344
1922		
USA	33,993	651,147
Guatemala	79	1,050
Cuba	24	600
Total	34,096	652,797
1923		
USA	9,318	251,327
Guatemala	114	3,240
Total	9,432	254,567
1924		
USA	14,354	342,151
Guatemala	201	5,300
Total	14,555	347,451
1925		
USA	38,837	988,760
Guatemala	62	6,825
British Honduras	10	600
Total	39,909	996,185
1926		
USA	98,043	4,481,824
Guatemala	101	2,530
Total	98,144	4,484,354
1927		
USA	131,132	4,374,424
Guatemala	9	1,090
Total	131,141	4,375,514
1928		
USA	112,062	7,234,361
Guatemala	6	500
Total	112,068	7,234,861
1929		
USA	179,367	7,295,042
Total	179,556	7,314,492

TABLE 3 (cont'd.)

Destination and Year	Quantity	Value
1930		
USA	173,035	8,219,698
Total	173,035	8,226,618
1931–1933		
USA (1931–1933)	67,500	1,278,204
Total	68,471	1,355,558

SOURCE: *Anuarios estadísticos de comercio exterior*, 1920–1935.

TABLE 4

Cattle Exported from Mexico, 1946–1960

Category and Year	Quantity	Value
1946		
Females		
To six years of age	46,877	4,668,559
Older than six years	48,696	4,928,632
Males		
One year of age	62,736	6,412,226
Older than one year	288,865	31,353,362
1947–1951—None	—	—
1952		
Cattle of all classes		
Colombia	27	50,603
United States	5,971	2,640,330
Total	5,998	2,690,933
Male cattle to 200 kilograms		
(all USA)	117,519	38,360,576
1953		
Females	113	170,626
200 kilograms	134,482	58,841,112
1954		
Females	3,895	1,332,573
200 kilograms	750	346,256
1955		
Females	475	152,252
Males	242,959	103,515,998

TABLE 4 (cont'd.)

Category and Year	Quantity	Value
1956		
Females	5,764	2,544,190
Males	105,038	47,805,487
1958		
Females		
To 250 kilograms	4,654	1,735,091
Over 250 kilograms	4,445	2,434,435
Males		
To 100 kilograms	300,360	118,188,931
Over 100 kilograms	3,407	843,738
1959		
Females		
To 250 kilograms	258	113,412
Over 250 kilograms	190	161,519
Males		
To 100 kilograms	630	364,349
100–250 kilograms	256,034	155,532,609
Over 250 kilograms	116,614	134,894,455

SOURCE: *Anuarios estadísticos de comercio exterior,* 1946–1959.
NOTE: Data not available for 1957.

TABLE 5
Cattle Imported to Mexico, 1946–1960, by Use

Use and Year	Quantity	Value
1946		
Breeding		
Brazil	327	1,028,872
USA	2,944	1,559,132
Total	3,305	2,648,334
Up to two years		
USA	2,017	968,560
Total	2,730	1,201,778
More than two years		
USA	1,009	400,861
El Salvador	1,786	302,531
Guatemala	1,409	499,609
Honduras	448	72,489
Total	4,652	1,275,490

TABLE 5 (cont'd.)

Use and Year	Quantity	Value
1947		
Slaughter (all USA)	501	202,259
Breeding (all USA)	360	1,303,491
1948		
Slaughter		
USA	2	200
British Honduras	10	4,200
Total	12	4,400
Breeding		
Canada	19	9,588
USA	1,187	1,293,903
Total	1,206	1,303,491
1949		
Slaughter (all USA)	14	2,841
Fighting (all USA)	1	6,488
Breeding	1,003	1,595,804
1950		
Slaughter		
British Honduras	36	8,094
USA	10	9,466
Total	46	17,560
Breeding		
USA	610	1,079,060
Canada	31	17,810
Total	641	1,253,970
1951		
Slaughter (all USA)	4	1,700
Breeding		
Canada	62	307,409
USA	549	2,004,327
Total	611	
1952		
Slaughter		
USA	56	57,539
British Honduras	2	410
Total	58	57,949
Breeding		
Canada	35	174,730
Cuba	2	1,730
USA	1,549	3,939,965
Total	1,602	4,169,623

TABLE 5 (cont'd.)

Use and Year	Quantity	Value
1953		
Breeding	3,814	6,794,762
Slaughter	19	4,482
1954		
Slaughter	—	—
Breeding	1,949	4,315,006
1956		
Breeding	10,430	23,036,796
Slaughter	1	1,288
1957		
Breeding	23,172	63,080,195
Slaughter	13	44,698
1958		
Breeding	5,950	22,134,365
Slaughter	2,764	12,850,396
1960		
Breeding	5,463	18,860,300
Dairy	3,259	13,212,664

SOURCE: *Anuarios estadísticos de comercio exterior*, 1946–1960.
NOTE: Data not available for 1955. Discrepancies between totals and numbers from individual countries derive from a statistically insignificant number of cattle imported from several other countries.

TABLE 6

Cattle Imports to Mexico, 1960–1970

Category and Year	Quantity	Value
1960		
Breeding	5,980	21,179,180
Dairy	4,695	17,362,834
1961		
Breeding	7,045	23,884,316
Dairy	5,431	19,349,138
1962		
Breeding	5,713	19,313,827
Dairy	6,187	25,135,137

TABLE 6 (cont'd.)

Category and Year	Quantity	Value
1963		
Breeding	4,883	17,126,300
Dairy	8,755	25,256,300
Slaughter	2	420
1964		
Breeding	5,735	18,605,094
Dairy	5,864	25,256,300
Slaughter	124	219,850
1965		
With pedigree	6,329	20,186,893
Without pedigree	14,122	4,758,836
1966		
With pedigree	5,849	28,267,166
Without pedigree	271	965,500
1967		
With pedigree	5,822	28,020,129
Without pedigree	16	73,345
1968		
With pedigree	5,132	26,326,813
Without pedigree	3	970
1969		
With pedigree	4,979	28,172,962
Without pedigree	1	220
1970		
With pedigree	2,848	15,171,421
Without pedigree	32	28,000

SOURCE: *Anuarios estadísticos de comercio exterior*, 1960–1970.

TABLE 7

Cattle Exported from Mexico, 1960–1970, by Sex and Weight

Category and Year	Quantity	Value
1960		
Females		
To 250 kilograms	143	113,412
Over 250 kilograms	34	29,912
Males		
To 100 kilograms	835	263,375
100–250 kilograms	318,293	163,742,892
Over 250 kilograms	76,348	70,662,353

TABLE 7 (cont'd.)

Category and Year	Quantity	Value
1961		
Females		
To 250 kilograms	316	189,988
Males		
To 100 kilograms	4,026	1,371,472
100–250 kilograms	424,004	191,913,184
Over 250 kilograms	121,316	101,844,903
1962		
Females		
To 250 kilograms	520	252,883
Over 250 kilograms	2	3,500
Males		
To 100 kilograms	6,571	1,921,577
100–250 kilograms	624,267	275,188,684
Over 250 kilograms	121,316	109,879,665
1963		
Females		
To 250 kilograms	22	15,844
Over 250 kilograms	73	78,648
Males		
To 100 kilograms	7,969	2,609,290
100–250 kilograms	481,889	201,020,464
Over 250 kilograms	62,943	50,368,046
1964		
Females		
Over 250 kilograms	43	24,258
Males		
To 100 kilograms	5,141	1,623,683
100–250 kilograms	334,808	158,569,928
Over 250 kilograms	17,913	14,967,111
1965		
Females		
Over 250 kilograms	12	16,254
Males		
To 100 kilograms	3,636	1,794,540
100–250 kilograms	481,952	241,308,055
Over 250 kilograms	71,839	61,514,018
1966		
Females		
To 250 kilograms	938	374,200
Over 250 kilograms	10	10,000

TABLE 7 (cont'd.)

Category and Year	Quantity	Value
Males		
To 100 kilograms	8,460	2,415,401
100–250 kilograms	517,491	218,917,775
Over 250 kilograms	62,586	39,815,022
1967		
Females		
To 250 kilograms	22	21,824
Over 250 kilograms	73	93,110
Males		
To 100 kilograms	4,617	1,280,173
100–250 kilograms	510,871	223,632,192
Over 250 kilograms	8,570	7,223,916
1968		
Females		
Over 250 kilograms	358	863,400
Males		
To 100 kilograms	4,409	1,305,080
100–250 kilograms	687,496	308,661,119
Over 250 kilograms	18,617	15,599,545
1969		
Females		
Over 250 kilograms	374	714,691
Males		
To 100 kilograms	8,545	2,394,024
100–250 kilograms	817,971	361,459,309
Over 250 kilograms	13,467	9,748,487
1970		
Females		
To 250 kilograms	125,231	54,934,507
Over 250 kilograms	364	394,218
Males		
To 100 kilograms	7,614	2,251,616
100–250 kilograms	787,801	322,387,575
Over 250 kilograms	12,574	5,982,434

SOURCE: *Anuarios estadísticos de comercio exterior*, 1960–1970.

TABLE 8

Mexican Cattle Imported and Exported by the United States, 1969–1977

Category and Year	Imported	Exported
1969		
Quantity*	810	14
Value**	66.043	5.377
1970		
Quantity	937	9
Value	78.343	3.613
1971		
Quantity	752	12
Value	72.726	4.958
1972		
Quantity	916	17
Value	106.781	8.308
1973		
Quantity	673	31
Value	104.198	16.960
1974		
Quantity	435	62
Value	67.783	27.426
1975		
Quantity	196	116
Value	25.058	32.008
1976		
Quantity	508	92
Value	60.961	33.130
1977		
Quantity	594	—
Value	80.185	15.864

SOURCE: *USDA Computer Printout Tables Supplied by the Foreign Demand and Competition Division of the Economics, Statistics, and Cooperatives Service,* January 31, 1979.

*Thousands.

**Millions of dollars.

TABLE 9

Total Cattle Slaughtered in Mexico, 1949–1960

Year	Quantity	Weight	Value
1949	870,232	130,572,012	275,716,525
1950	941,984	143,688,163	326,737,514
1951	994,659	147,629,168	417,380,535
1952	1,031,434	154,090,619	514,679,650
1953	1,336,428	196,810,604	647,532,585
1955	1,378,010	206,452,980	889,372,009
1956	1,580,181	241,680,646	1,086,951,348
1957	1,728,280	252,671,820	1,210,449,663
1958	1,761,679	263,720,615	1,349,544,982
1959	1,735,543	264,609,010	1,427,932,575
1960	1,804,789	273,981,404	1,770,310,916

SOURCE: General Files, Dirección General de Estadística (Mexico City).
NOTE: Data not available for 1954.

TABLE 10

Cattle Slaughtered in Northern Mexico,
by State, 1949–1960

State and Year	Quantity	Weight	Value
Chihuahua			
1949	46,071	6,289,478	12,055,878
1950	55,680	8,496,017	16,958,643
1951	52,071	7,242,351	20,067,024
1952	61,006	7,989,888	22,309,483
1953	81,885	11,246,183	34,131,820
1955	61,196	8,256,328	36,170,324
1956	70,181	9,607,621	47,104,197
1957	80,483	11,681,362	60,343,464
1958	77,396	11,151,998	61,634,219
1959	72,750	11,533,452	73,223,550
1960	81,078	13,021,522	90,657,495
Coahuila			
1949	32,086	4,423,297	8,512,118
1950	36,865	4,823,861	9,240,496
1951	45,980	6,294,927	14,555,690

TABLE 10 (cont'd.)

State and Year	Quantity	Weight	Value
1952	34,464	4,270,968	12,594,296
1953	45,289	5,524,772	18,594,531
1955	35,981	5,034,700	22,477,712
1956	38,529	5,519,794	26,884,806
1957	47,803	4,892,224	28,536,450
1958	41,224	5,595,622	33,881,061
1959	34,638	4,870,088	27,333,232
1960	38,402	5,315,712	32,307,181
Federal District			
1949	211,383	32,973,027	65,073,890
1950	229,015	36,185,454	80,811,417
1951	230,893	36,045,317	94,133,491
1952	239,604	37,908,053	119,800,731
1953	254,727	40,578,340	121,018,717
1955	264,408	42,248,419	171,556,521
1956	419,422	64,739,990	278,621,538
1957	506,373	77,283,899	325,365,123
1958	534,398	82,719,803	350,896,407
1959	512,130	78,425,604	330,758,016
1960	498,882	75,971,421	470,879,812
Durango			
1949	17,514	2,608,008	4,581,195
1950	19,382	2,829,783	4,916,519
1951	20,087	2,658,046	6,035,482
1952	21,154	2,713,217	7,298,916
1953	32,355	4,285,562	11,949,092
1955	29,625	4,157,174	16,345,826
1956	30,107	4,430,974	19,356,525
1957	31,617	4,194,904	20,618,530
1958	28,463	3,816,209	19,616,400
1959	23,743	3,229,260	21,731,041
1960	26,628	3,480,314	20,859,500
Nuevo León			
1949	43,443	6,563,976	11,103,679
1950	45,626	7,179,838	12,693,470
1951	40,038	7,728,028	20,727,162
1952	58,520	7,571,435	26,681,961
1953	60,564	7,291,581	24,212,962
1955	58,864	7,225,786	29,601,732
1956	60,479	7,662,541	26,223,541

TABLE 10 (cont'd.)

State and Year	Quantity	Weight	Value
1957	62,584	6,331,640	33,341,467
1958	67,969	7,225,786	29,601,732
1959	70,323	11,772,933	67,430,018
1960	77,292	12,421,447	80,886,598
Sonora			
1949	46,576	5,698,541	15,717,488
1950	48,436	6,039,749	19,178,627
1951	54,278	6,792,884	24,759,757
1952	57,424	6,957,426	29,837,658
1953	75,733	9,369,572	34,931,652
1955	81,706	10,041,884	55,010,837
1956	83,315	10,009,440	34,619,757
1957	90,120	10,605,070	64,625,031
1958	81,573	9,851,550	66,888,163
1959	79,790	9,969,363	72,783,660
1960	88,775	11,478,614	90,865,681
Tamaulipas			
1949	39,009	6,815,240	13,990,216
1950	46,916	7,365,324	18,705,237
1951	53,936	8,087,664	24,760,943
1952	61,092	9,121,237	32,798,777
1953	64,537	9,449,666	34,024,893
1955	78,580	11,110,616	49,119,263
1956	78,082	11,190,863	55,277,010
1957	80,381	11,411,257	56,697,796
1958	90,175	10,947,881	77,168,130
1959	88,323	12,479,179	76,371,819
1960	92,503	13,119,233	86,537,286

SOURCE: General Files, Dirección General de Estadística (Mexico City).
NOTE: Data not available for 1954.

TABLE 11

National Pastureland, 1930–1960

	1930	1940	1950	1960
More than five hectares	62,935,524	45,430,261	50,765,846	59,442,529
Less than five hectares*		83,095	82,984	356,759
Ejidos	3,557,279	10,658,915	16,530,212	19,613,988

SOURCE: Dirección General de Estadística, *I, II, III, and IV censos agrícolas y ganaderos 1930, 1940, 1950, and 1960.*
* Data not available for 1930.

TABLE 12

Pasturelands in Northern Mexico, 1930–1960

Location and Category	1930	1940	1950	1960
Chihuahua				
More than five hectares	13,548,236	12,749,352	14,555,353	13,010,287.9
Less than five hectares*		350	161	308.2
Ejidos	754,996	1,537,188	2,328,043	2,946,404.5
Coahuila				
More than five hectares	9,685,141	8,142,276	7,518,451	8,646,517.7
Less than five hectares*		156	208	310.0
Ejidos	94,426	682,097	763,469	1,140,868.2
Sonora				
More than five hectares	4,863,804	4,241,659	6,297,742	8,785,866.6
Less than five hectares*		199	343	134.6
Ejidos	144,547	493,894	890,860	1,026,829.8
Total Northern States				
More than five hectares**	42,444,735	30,357,828	30,972,382	30,422,672.2
Less than five hectares*		15,404	14,685	652.8
Ejidos	2,117,920	6,106,675	8,433,022	5,114,102.6

SOURCE: Dirección General de Estadística, *I, II, III, and IV censos agrícolas y ganaderos 1930, 1940, 1950, and 1960.*
NOTE: Included are Chihuahua, Coahuila, Durango, Nuevo León, Sonora, Zacatecas, San Luis Potosí, and Tamaulipas.
* None in 1930.
** Includes only 1960 totals for Sonora, Coahuila, and Chihuahua.

Bibliography

Archival Materials

Mexico

Archivo Histórico de la Secretaría de Relaciones Exteriores, Tlatelolco, D.F.

Camargo Núñez, Fernando. Personal Archives. Mexico City.

Dirección General de Estadística. General Files, Mexico City.

Dirección General Ganadería. "Plan para el mejoramiento genético mediante el canje de bovinos corrientes por sementales de raza pura." Supplied to the author, April, 1972.

Secretaría de Agricultura y Ganadería. "Las enfermedades de los animales domésticos como factor limitante en la producción pecuaria en México." Manuscript supplied by the Dirección de Sanidad Animàl. Mexico City. April, 1972.

United States

Buckley, W. F. Papers. University of Texas Archives. Austin.

National Archives, Washington, D.C.

    Record Group 17. U.S. Department of Agriculture. Records of the Bureau of Animal Industry, 1910–1939.

    Record Group 59. U.S. Department of State. Papers of the Department of State Relating to the Internal Affairs of Mexico, 1910–1929.

    Record Group 156. U.S. Department of Commerce. Records of the Bureau of Foreign and Domestic Commerce.

    Record Group 166. U.S. Department of Agriculture. Records of the Bureau of Foreign Agricultural Relations.

National Association for the Protection of American Rights in Mexico. Papers. University of Texas Archives. Austin.

Pryor, Ike T. Papers, Speeches. University of Texas Archives, Austin.

Records of the Adjutant General. Texas Ranger Correspondence. Texas State Archives. Austin.
Texas and Southwestern Cattlemen's Association. Papers. University of Texas Archives. Austin.
U.S. Department of Agriculture. Files of the Agricultural History Branch. Washington, D.C.

Government Publications

Mexico

Anuarios estadísticos de comercio exterior. 1920–. Mexico City: Talleres Gráficos de la Nación.
Banco Nacional de Crédito Agrícola y Ganadero. *Veinticinco Años del Banco Nacional de Crédito Agrícola y Ganadero.* Mexico City, 1951.
Banco Nacional de Mexico. "Some Aspects of Mexican Stock Raising." Examen de la Situación Económica de México, vol. 32, pp. 8–13. Mexico City, 1956.
Comisión contra la Fiebre Aftosa. *La campaña contra la fiebre aftosa.* Mexico City, 1949.
———. *La fiebre aftosa en México (Estado actual de la campaña).* Mexico City, 1951.
———. *Investigación científica de la fiebre aftosa de México.* Mexico City, 1948.
———. *Programa para la erradicación de la fiebre aftosa.* Mexico City, 1948.
Comité de Fomento Agropecuario del Norte. *Temario: Estudio social, económico y ecológico de la ganadería de México.* Chihuahua City: Unión Regional Ganadera de Chihuahua, 1964.
Dirección General de Estadística. *I, II, III, and IV Censos Agrícolas y Ganaderos, 1930, 1940, 1950, and 1960.* Mexico City, 1935, 1951, 1956, and 1965.
———. *Estadística ganadera de la Republica.* Mexico City: Secretaría de Fomento, 1903.
Secretaría de Agricultura y Ganadería. *Cría y explotación del ganado bovino.* Mexico City: Subsecretaría de Ganadería, 1969.

United States

California, State of. Senate. *First, Second, Third Reports on Foot and Mouth Disease. Partial Report of Senate Interim Committee on Livestock Diseases.* Sacramento, 1948, 1949, 1951.
Congressional Record
Davis, Floyd E., and George J. Dietz. *Beef Cattle in Northern Mexico and Probable Exports to the United States.* U.S. Department of Agriculture. Foreign Agriculture Report 69, August, 1952.

Salmon, D. E. *Mexico as a Market for Purebred Beef Cattle from the United States.* Bureau of Animal Industry Bulletin No. 41. Washington, D.C.: Government Printing Office, 1902.

U.S. Congress. House. 80th Congress, 2d session, February 26, 1948. House Report 1425.

—————. Committee on Agriculture. *Eradication of Foot and Mouth Disease: Hearings before a Subcommittee of the House Committee on Agriculture.* 80th Congress, 1st session, December 3, 4, and 5, 1947.

—————. Subcommittee on Foot and Mouth Disease of the Committee on Agriculture. *The Campaign against Foot and Mouth Disease.* 80th Congress, 1st session, July 17, 1947.

U.S. Congress. Senate. Subcommittee to the Committee on Appropriations. *Control of Foot and Mouth Disease.* 80th Congress, 2d session, 1948. Senate Document 211.

U.S. Department of Agriculture. *Computer Printout Tables Supplied by the Foreign Demand and Competition Division of the Economics, Statistics, and Cooperative Service.* January 31, 1979.

—————. "Foot-and-Mouth Disease." *Farmers' Bulletin* No. 666. Washington, D.C., 1952.

—————. Animal and Plant Health Inspection Service. *Progress in Screwworm Eradication.* Washington, D.C., 1976.

U.S. Department of State. *Eradication of Foot-and-Mouth Disease in Mexico.* Treaties and Other International Acts, Series 2404. Washington, D.C.: Government Printing Office, 1953.

—————. *Papers Relating to the Foreign Relations of the United States, 1917. The American Republics.* Washington, D.C.: Government Printing Office, 1926.

Interviews

Camargo Núñez, Fernando. July, 1962. Mexico City.

De la Torre Zarza, Dr. Luis. Director of Vaccine Production, Comisión México-Americana para la Prevención de la Fiebre Aftosa. June 25, 1963. Mexico City.

Lewis, Cecil. Los Angeles County Livestock Department. September 11, 1961.

Major, Dr. Fred J. Inspector, Animal Disease Eradication, U.S. Department of Agriculture. El Paso, Texas. July 16, 1962.

Schroeder, Dr. Robert J. Director, Los Angeles County Livestock Department. September 11, 1961. Los Angeles, California.

Williams, Dr. Donald L. Codirector, Mexican-American Commission for the Prevention of Foot-and-Mouth Disease. July 22, 1962. Mexico City.

Newspapers

Diario Oficial, Mexico City.
El Diario, Chihuahua City.
El Universal, Mexico City.
Excelsior, Mexico City.
La Prensa, Mexico City.
New York Times.
New York *Sun.*
Novedades, Mexico City.
Ultimas Noticias, Mexico City.

Books

Almada, Francisco R. *La revolución en el estado de Chihuahua.* 2 vols. Mexico City: Biblioteca del Instituto Nacional de Estudios Históricos de la Revolución Mexicana, 1964. This is a basic study of the Revolution in Mexico's largest state.

Atkin, Ronald. *Revolution! Mexico, 1910–1920.* New York: John Day Co., 1969.

Auró Saldaña, Ramón. *Factores que han influído en la extensión y la propagación de la fiebre aftosa en nuestro país.* Mexico City: Escuela Nacional de Medicina Veterinaria y Zoötecnica, Universidad Nacional Autónoma Mexicana, 1947. A basic work for the understanding of medical as well as cultural aspects of the foot-and-mouth disease problem.

Brandenburg, Frank. *The Making of Modern Mexico.* Englewood Cliffs, N.J.: Prentice-Hall, 1964. This work presents a good, systematic analysis of institutionalization in Mexico to the early 1960's.

Clendenen, Clarence C. *The United States and Pancho Villa: A Study in Unconventional Diplomacy.* Ithaca: Cornell University Press, 1961.

Cline, Howard F. *The United States and Mexico.* New York: Atheneum, 1963. A basic study of United States–Mexican relations.

Cossío Silva, Luis. "La Ganadería." In Daniel Cosío Villegas, ed., *Historia moderna de México,* vol. VI, *El Porfiriato,* pt. 1, *La vida economica,* pp. 153–154. Mexico City: Editorial Hermes, 1965.

Cumberland, Charles C. *Mexican Revolution: The Constitutionalist Years.* Austin: University of Texas Press, 1972. This work covers in almost epic form the struggle against Huerta and the final dominance of Carranza in Mexico.

Fuentes Mares, José. . . . *Y México se refugió en el desierto: Luis Terrazas, historia y destino.* Mexico City: Editorial Jus, 1954. So far, this is the nearest thing available to a biography of Luis Terrazas.

Garza Buentello, Javier. *Administración de fincas ganaderas.* Mexico City: Herrero Hnos, Sucesores, 1966.

Gilderhus, Mark T. *Diplomacy and Revolution: United States–Mexican Relations under Wilson and Carranza.* Tucson: University of Arizona Press, 1977. A concise study of diplomacy during the most intense period of the Mexican Revolution.

Gómez, Marte R. *La reforma agraria en las filas villistas, años 1913 a 1915 y 1920.* Mexico City: Biblioteca del Instituto Nacional de Estudios Históricos de la Revolución Mexicana, 1966. A work essential to an understanding of villista concepts of land reform.

Gipson, Fred, and Bill Leftwich. *The "Cow Killers": With the Aftosa Commission in Mexico.* Austin: University of Texas Press, 1956. An entertaining view of a serious problem.

Lewis, Oscar. *The Children of Sánchez.* New York: Random House, 1961.

Lister, Florence C., and Robert H. Lister. *Chihuahua: Storehouse of Storms.* Albuquerque: University of New Mexico Press, 1966. A good view from the perspective of cultural geography and history of the role of Chihuahua in Mexico. The Listers also present a balanced view of the cattle industry.

López Rosado, Diego G. *Historia y pensamiento económico de México.* I, *Agricultura y ganadería: Propiedad de la tierra.* Mexico City: Universidad Nacional Autónoma Mexicana, 1968.

Machado, Manuel A., Jr. *AFTOSA: Foot-and-Mouth Disease and Inter-American Relations.* Albany: State University of New York Press, 1969.

————. *An Industry in Crisis: Mexican–United States Cooperation in the Control of Foot-and-Mouth Disease.* Berkeley: University of California Press, 1968.

Martínez, Oscar J. *Border Boom Town: Ciudad Juárez since 1848.* Austin: University of Texas Press, 1978. Offers little about the cattle industry in Chihuahua although there are some interesting interpretations on the dependency of Juárez on El Paso.

Meyer, Michael C. *Huerta: A Political Portrait.* Lincoln: University of Nebraska Press, 1972.

————. *Mexican Rebel: Pascual Orozco and the Mexican Revolution, 1910–1915.* Lincoln: University of Nebraska Press, 1967.

Mollin, F. E. *The Outbreak of Foot and Mouth Disease in Mexico.* Denver: American National Livestock Association, 1947. A contemporary view of the aftosa problem.

Porter, James A. *Doctor, Spare My Cow.* Ames, Iowa: Iowa State College Press, 1956. A good firsthand account of events during the anti-aftosa campaign.

Quesada Bravo, Guillermo. *La verdad sobre el ganado cebú brasileño, la fiebre aftosa y la cuarentena en la Isla de Sacrificios.* Mexico City: n.p., 1946. Basically a defense of his position as director of husbandry when the Zebus arrived in Mexico in 1945 and 1946.

Quirk, Robert E. *The Mexican Revolution, 1914–1915: The Convention at Aguascalientes*. Bloomington: Indiana University Press, 1961.

Reeves, Frank. *Hacienda de Atotonilco*. Yerbanis, Durango: Atotonilco Livestock Company, 1936.

Reina Celaya, Alfonso. *La industria de la carne en México*. Mexico City: Imprenta A. Canalizo, 1958.

Seltzer, R. E., and T. M. Stubblefield. *Marketing Mexican Cattle in the United States*. Technical Bulletin No. 142. Tucson: University of Arizona Press, 1960.

United Nations. Comisión Económica para América Latina. *La industria de la carne de ganado bovino en México. Analisis y perspectivas*. Mexico City: Fondo de Cultura Económica, 1975.

Whetten, Nathan L. *Rural Mexico*. Chicago: University of Chicago Press, 1948. A fundamental book for understanding village organization in Mexico.

Wilkie, James W. *The Mexican Revolution: Federal Expenditure and Social Change*. Berkeley: University of California Press, 1970. Offers very little about the cattle industry.

Periodicals

Alanís Patiño, Emilio. "La industria de la carne en México." *Problemas agrícolas e industriales de México* 4 (July–September, 1952): 231–301.

American Brahman Journal.

American Cattle Producer.

Confederación Nacional Ganadera. *México ganadero*.

Brand, Donald D. "The Early History of the Range Cattle Industry in Northern Mexico." *Agricultural History* 35 (July, 1962): 132–139. This is an indispensable introductory study of the cattle industry of northern Mexico.

"El crédito a la ganadería en México." *Revista de economía continental* 2 (January, 1947): 17–26.

Dobie, James Frank. "Babícora." *American Hereford Journal* 44 (January 1, 1954): 56–60, 174–175.

Duckworth, C. U. "Cooperación internacional en vasta escala, una realidad demostrada en el control de la fiebre aftosa." *Pan American Sanitary Bureau Bulletin* 31 (September, 1951): 244–247.

"El ganado vacuno." *Monografías comerciales: Boletín mensual de la dirección rural* 227 (April, 1945): 204–239.

Hopkins, John A. "Fight against Hoof-and-Mouth Disease in Mexico." *Agriculture in the Americas* 7 (June–July, 1947).

Journal of the American Veterinary Medical Association.

Koch, Charles R. "Beef below the Border." *Farm Quarterly* 24 (Summer, 1969): 44–49.

López Portillo, Arturo. "La industria frigorífica en México." *Revista de economía* 8 (June, 1945): 11–13.

Machado, Manuel A., Jr. "*Aftosa* and the Mexican–United States Sanitary Convention of 1928." *Agricultural History* 39 (October, 1965): 240–245.

————. "The Mexican Revolution and the Destruction of the Mexican Cattle Industry." *Southwestern Historical Quarterly* 79 (July, 1975): 1–20.

Peffer, E. Louise. "Foot-and-Mouth Disease in United States Policy." *Food Research Institute Studies* 3 (May, 1962). Stanford University.

Sims, Harold D. "Espejo de caciques: Los Terrazas de Chihuahua." *Historia Mexicana* 18 (January–March, 1969): 379–399.

Smith, Mervin G. "The Mexican Beef Cattle Industry." *Foreign Agriculture* 8 (November, 1944).

Index

Aberdeen Angus cattle, 59, 108, 109
aftosa. *See* foot-and-mouth disease
Agrarian Code: of 1922, 39; of 1925, 34
agrarian laws, 36, 48. *See also* agrarian reform; land laws
agrarian reform: in Chihuahua, 13; in Coahuila, 51; constitutional mandate for, 24–25, 47; effects of, 56–57, 120; government commitment to, 49, 100–101, 119; pressures for, 33, 35, 50; tempering of, 35, 36, 54
agraristas, 13, 34, 43; oppose Terrazas sale, 44
Agricultural Research Foundation, 113
Aguascalientes, Convention of, 12–13
Alemán, Miguel: aids CMAPEFA, 75–76, 88; alleged corruption of, 100; and cattle industry, 94–95
Alemán–Ortiz Garza Plan, 71
anaplasmosis, 62
anthrax, 36, 47, 63–64
Article 27: effects of, 24–25, 33; defines land tenure, 24–25
artificial insemination, 79, 102, 107
Asociación Nacional de Productores de Leche Pura (National Association of Milk Producers), 81–82

Babícora Ranch, 50; expropriation of, threatened, 20, 34–36; losses of, 31; settlement of dispute over, 101; size of, 34–35
Baja California, 11, 111
Banco Nacional de Crédito Agrícola, 40, 59, 103
Banco Nacional de Crédito Ejidal, 59

beef: canned, 75, 95; consumption of, 38, 59, 60–61, 97–98, 104; demand for, 105, 110, 119, 121. *See also* meat
Bell, Raymond, 53–54, 58
blackleg, 64
border inspection, 73, 75, 81
bovine tuberculosis, 36
brand inspection, 18
Brangus cattle, 109
Brazil: and Zebu controversy, 67–70
breed improvement. *See* breeding stock; cattle, improvement of
breeding stock: export of, prohibited, 111; government encourages purchase of, 39, 121; need to import, 38, 47; from South America, 121; from U.S., 48, 96, 103, 107, 118, 121
bribery, 23, 37, 90, 106
Bureau of Animal Industry, 16, 30, 37, 65, 81

Calles, Plutarco Elías, 33, 35, 50
Camargo Nuñez, Fernando, 70, 71
campesinos: reaction of, to foot-and-mouth disease, 71, 80, 82–88
Cananea Cattle Company, 52, 53
canneries, 75, 95
Cárdenas, Lázaro: contribution of, to cattle industry, 120–121; decree of unaffectability of, 54–55; rise to power of, 49–52
Carothers, George C., 15, 16–17
carrancistas: seizure of cattle by, 10–11
Carranza, Venustiano: breaks with

Villa, 11–13; moves against foreign holdings, 24; pronounces against Huerta, 10; recognized by U.S., 18; sells cattle, 21; taxes foreign-owned cattle, 20–21

cattle: confiscation of, 9–13 passim, 18–22 passim, 30–31 (see also rustling); compensation for loss of, 72, 73–74; costs of production of, 58, 102; decline in population of, 29; improvement of, 7–8, 58–59, 95–97, 101–102, 107, 109; increase of, 99, 101, 109–110; losses of, 24, 31–32; markets for, 27, 30, 48, 58–59, 94, 95, 97, 104, 116, 121

cattle industry: changes in, 5, 119; culture of, 122–123, 124; effects of disease on, 95 (see also specific diseases); efforts to rebuild, 33, 53–54; financing of, 40, 59, 102–103; government attitude toward, 40, 50–51, 54, 62, 103, 107; growth of, 7, 65–66, 102–104; and Mexican economy, 122; modernization of, 92–93, 107, 108; problems of, 29–30, 39–40, 117

cattlemen: conservatism of, 122, 123; organization of, 40, 57–58, 62, 108–109, 111; reaction of, to Cárdenas, 51–53; and Revolution, 21, 23–24, 119; and Zebu bulls, 69

Cattle Raisers Association of Texas, 18

cattle scab, 63, 64

Charolais cattle, 109

Chiapas, 76, 109

Chihuahua, 32, 62; agrarian code of, 35, 39, 41, 43; agriculture in, 42; beef consumption in, 98; cattle in, 7, 59, 108–109, 111; early settlement of, 3; exports of, 107–108; expropriation in, 35–36, 55; imports of, 101; livestock association in, 57; livestock exhibitions in, 108–109; pastures in, 99–100; revolutionary activity in, 6, 9, 12, 13, 19; traditionalism of, 108–109; U.S. owners in, 33

Ciudad Juárez, 22; slaughterhouse at, 14–18; shipping at, 111

Coahuila, 32; beef consumption in, 98; cattle in, 7; land law of, 51; revolutionary activity in, 23

Cobb, Zack: and Villa, 16, 17–18, 19, 22; and Palomas cattle, 23

Columbus, N.M.: raid on, 20

Comisión México–Americana para la Erradicación de la Fiebre Aftosa (CMAPEFA): changes name, 82; creation of, 72; early activities of, 72–73; laboratory facilities of, 78–80; problems of, 75; rigorous inspection by, 81

Comisión México–Americana para la Prevención de la Fiebra Aftosa (CMAPPFA): creation of, 82

Comisión Nacional Agraria (National Agrarian Commission): activities of, in Chihuahua, 13, 41; cattlemen criticize, 52; expropriates Corralitas lands, 34

Companía Agraria de Chihuahua, 41, 42

Companía Agrícola y Ganadera de San Carlo, 23

Confederación Nacional Ganadera, 57, 114, 120–121

constitutionalistas: defined, 10 n. 12; debts of, 22; and export tax, 21

Constitution of 1917: agrarian mandates of, 24–25, 33, 50; cattlemen and, 119, 123

contraband, 23–24

Corralitas Land and Cattle Company: breed improvement by, 7–8; threatened expropriation of, 34

corruption, 13, 90–91

credit, 59, 102, 103

criollo cattle: improvement of, 7, 58, 101, 107; percentage of, 108; in ejido herds, 117

derriengue, 112

Díaz, Porfirio, 5–9

dipping, 26, 37, 62–63, 65

Dirección General de Investigaciones Pecuarias, 75, 112, 114

disease: cattlemen combat, 62; spread of, 64–65. See also Mexican–United